Pennsylvania Railroad to the Columbian Exposition

Marula

An imprint of Arcadia Publishing

Pennsylvania Railroad to the Columbian Exposition
with Descriptive Notes of the Cities of New York, Washington, Philadelphia,
Chicago, and a Complete Description of the Exposition Grounds and Buildings

Pennsylvania Railroad Company

A Marula Historical Reprint
Originally published in 1892

Published by Arcadia Publishing
Charleston SC

ISBN 978-0-7385-9474-3

Printed in the United States of America

For all general information contact Arcadia Publishing at:
Telephone 843-853-2070
Fax 843-853-0044
E-mail sales@arcadiapublishing.com
For customer service and orders:
Toll-Free 1-888-313-2665

Visit us on the Internet at www.arcadiapublishing.com

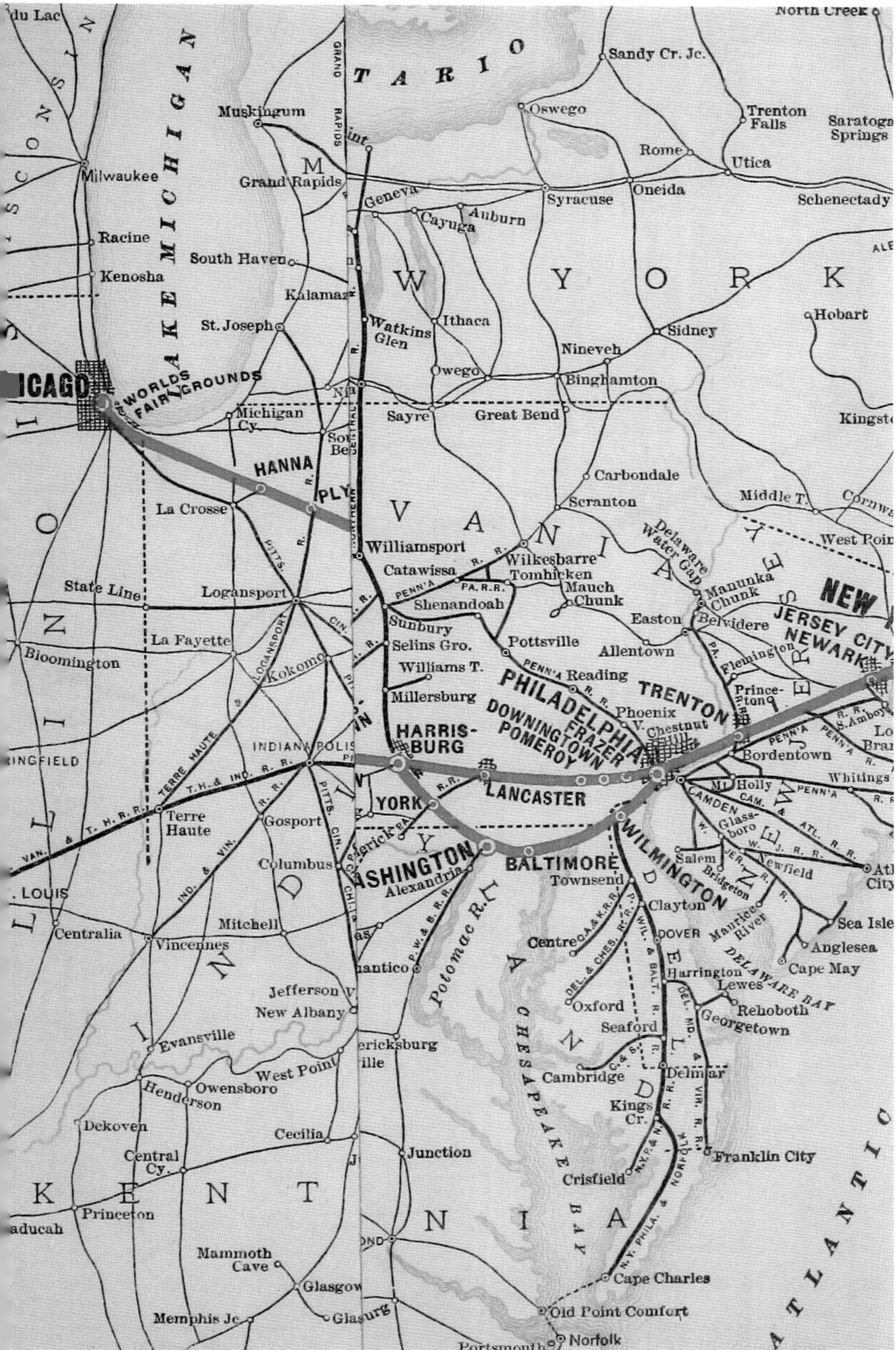

LAKE MICHIGAN
ONTARIO
NEW YORK
PENNSYLVANIA
NEW JERSEY
MARYLAND
DELAWARE
VIRGINIA
INDIANA
ILLINOIS
KENTUCKY
WISCONSIN
ATLANTIC
CHICAGO
WORLDS FAIR GROUNDS
HANNA
PLY
HARRISBURG
PHILADELPHIA
DOWNINGTOWN
FRAZER
POMEROY
LANCASTER
YORK
BALTIMORE
WASHINGTON
WILMINGTON
TRENTON
JERSEY CITY
NEWARK
NEW
Milwaukee
Racine
Kenosha
Muskingum
Grand Rapids
South Haven
Kalamazoo
St. Joseph
Michigan Cy.
La Crosse
Logansport
La Fayette
Kokomo
State Line
Bloomington
Indianapolis
Terre Haute
Gosport
Columbus
Centralia
Vincennes
Mitchell
Jefferson V.
New Albany
Evansville
Henderson
Owensboro
West Point
Dekoven
Central Cy.
Cecilia
Princeton
Mammoth Cave
Glasgow
Memphis Jc.
Oswego
Sandy Cr. Jc.
Trenton Falls
Saratoga Springs
North Creek
Rome
Utica
Syracuse
Oneida
Schenectady
Geneva
Auburn
Cayuga
Watkins Glen
Ithaca
Sidney
Hobart
Nineveh
Binghamton
Owego
Sayre
Great Bend
Carbondale
Scranton
Middle T.
West Point
Williamsport
Catawissa
Wilkesbarre
Tomhicken
Mauch Chunk
Shenandoah
Sunbury
Selins Gro.
Williams T.
Millersburg
Pottsville
Reading
Allentown
Easton
Delaware Water Gap
Manunka Chunk
Belvidere
Flemington
Princeton
Phoenix V.
Chestnut Hill
Bordentown
Mt. Holly
Whitings
Glassboro
Salem
Bridgeton
Newfield
Atlantic City
Sea Isle
Anglesea
Cape May
Maurice River
Delaware Bay
Alexandria
Townsend
Clayton
Dover
Centre
Harrington
Oxford
Lewes
Rehoboth
Georgetown
Seaford
Cambridge
Delmar
Kings Cr.
Franklin City
Crisfield
Chesapeake Bay
Potomac R.
Junction
Cape Charles
Old Point Comfort
Norfolk
Portsmouth

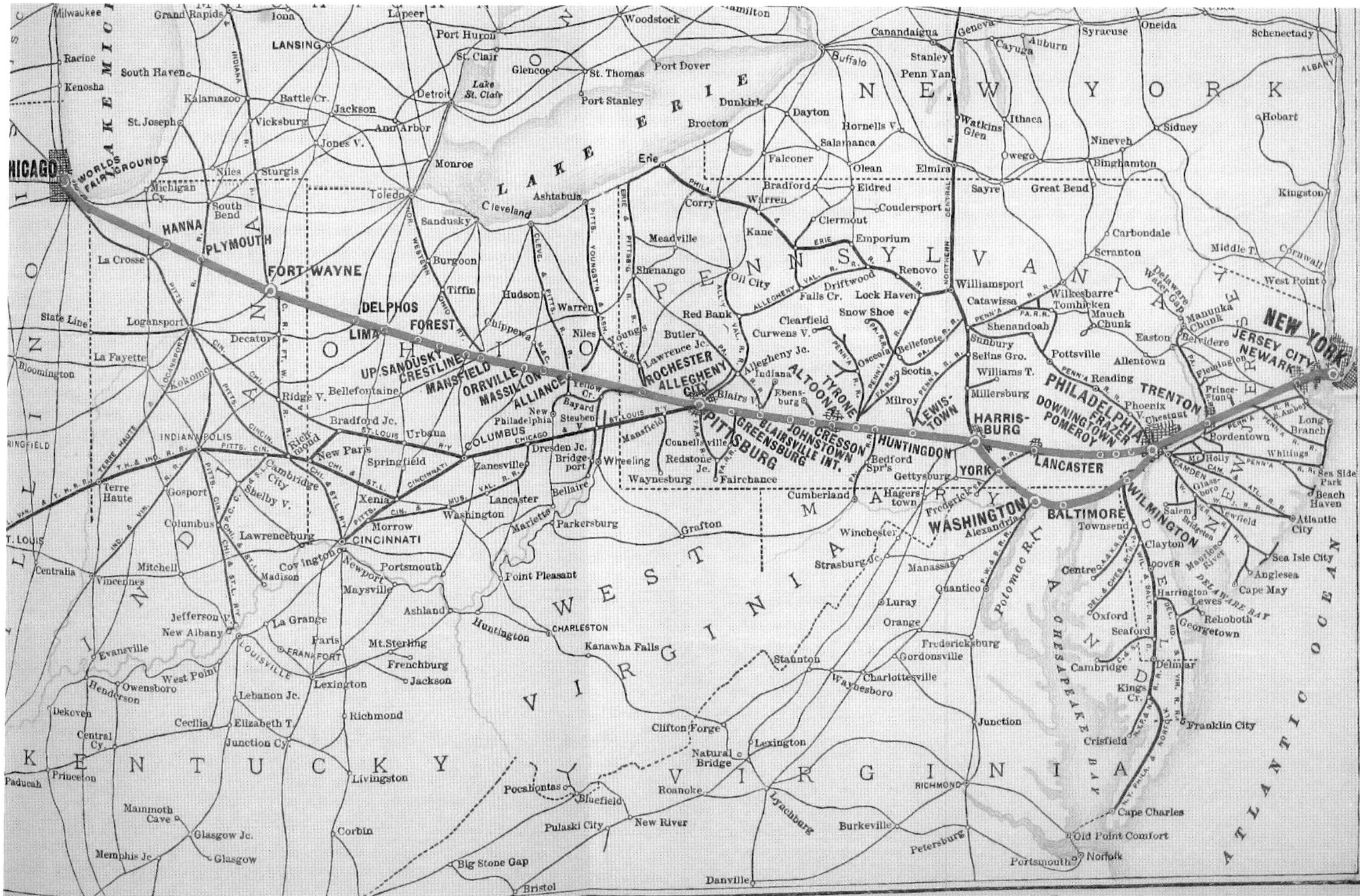

…ROAD NEW YORK TO CHICAGO.

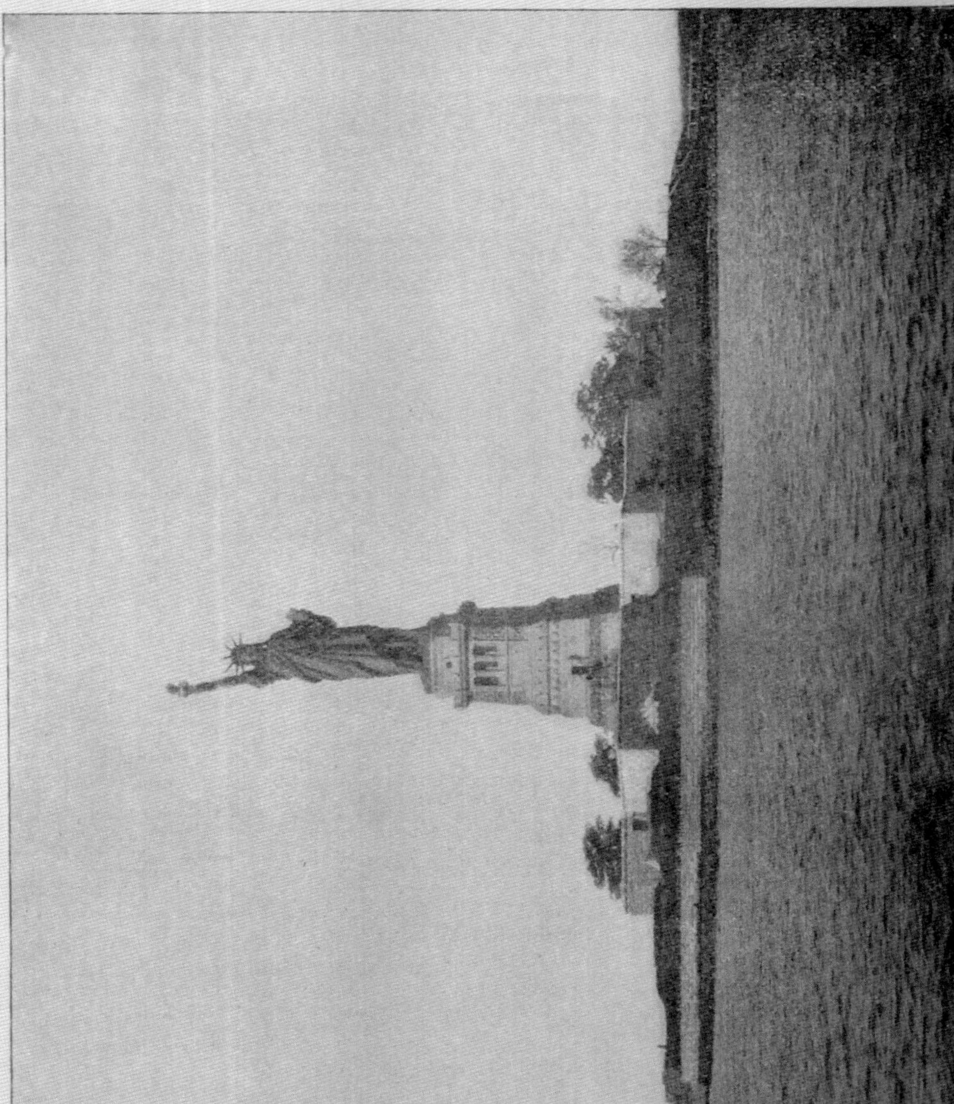

PENNSYLVANIA RAILROAD

TO THE

COLUMBIAN EXPOSITION,

WITH DESCRIPTIVE NOTES OF THE CITIES OF

NEW YORK, WASHINGTON,
PHILADELPHIA, CHICAGO,

AND A COMPLETE DESCRIPTION OF THE

EXPOSITION GROUNDS AND BUILDINGS,

WITH MAPS AND ILLUSTRATIONS.

PHILADELPHIA:
PENNSYLVANIA RAILROAD COMPANY.
1892.

Allen, Lane & Scott, Printers, Philadelphia, Pa.

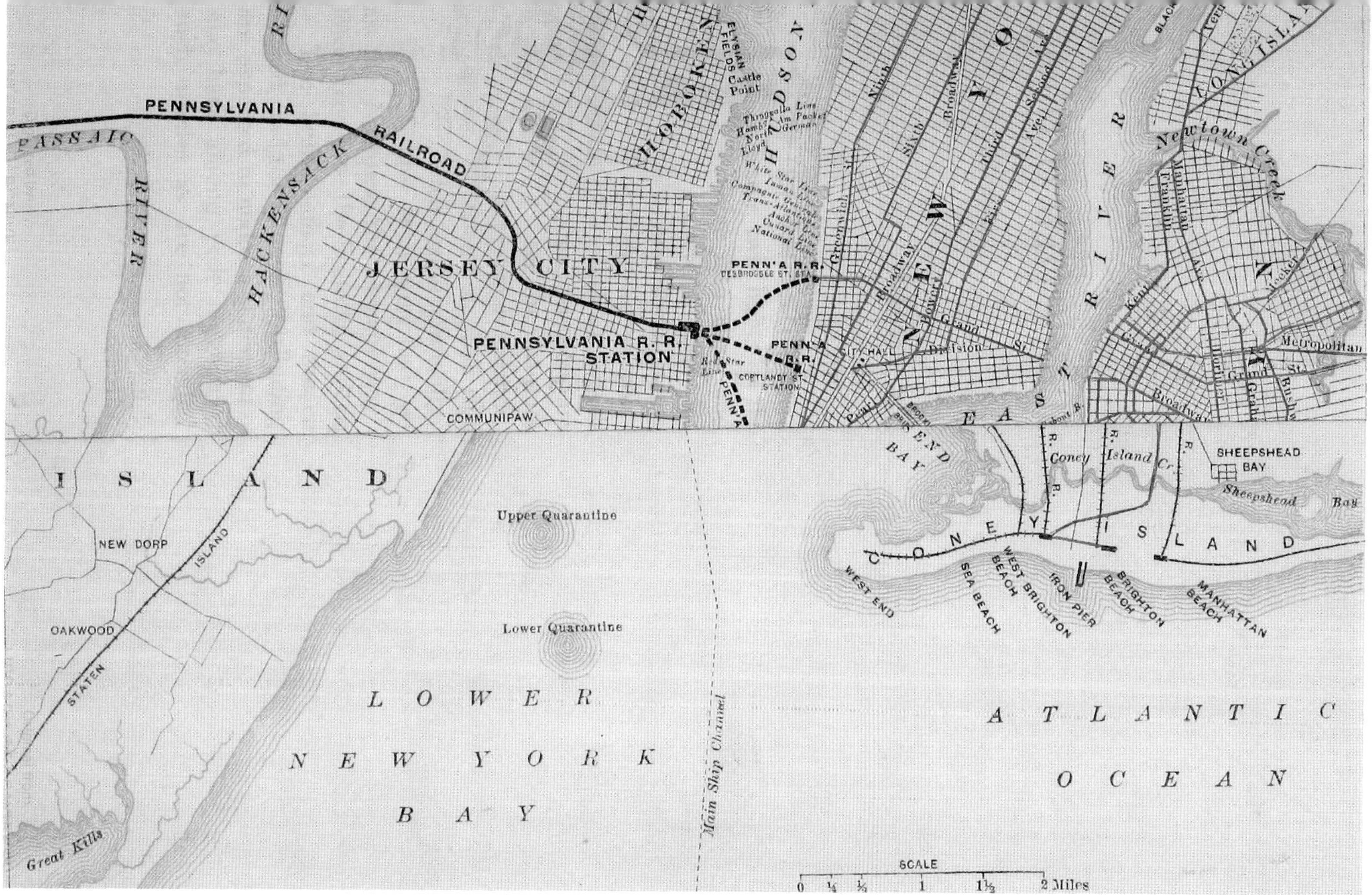
PENNSYLVANIA RAILROAD
PASSAIC RIVER
HACKENSACK
JERSEY CITY
HOBOKEN
ELYSIAN FIELDS
Castle Point
HUDSON
PENNSYLVANIA R. R. STATION
PENN'A R.R.
DESBROSSES ST. STA.
PENN'A R.R.
CORTLANDT ST. STATION
PENN'A
COMMUNIPAW
NEW YORK
EAST RIVER
Newtown Creek
LONG ISLAND
Broadway
Bowery
Grand St.
Division
CITY HALL
Greenwich
Ninth
Sixth
Third Ave.
Second Ave.
Manhattan
Franklin
Metropolitan
ISLAND
NEW DORP
OAKWOOD
STATEN ISLAND
Upper Quarantine
Lower Quarantine
LOWER NEW YORK BAY
Main Ship Channel
Great Kills
SHEEPSHEAD BAY
Sheepshead Bay
Coney Island Cr.
CONEY ISLAND
WEST END
SEA BEACH
WEST BRIGHTON BEACH
IRON PIER
BRIGHTON BEACH
MANHATTAN BEACH
ATLANTIC OCEAN
SCALE
0 ¼ ½ 1 1½ 2 Miles

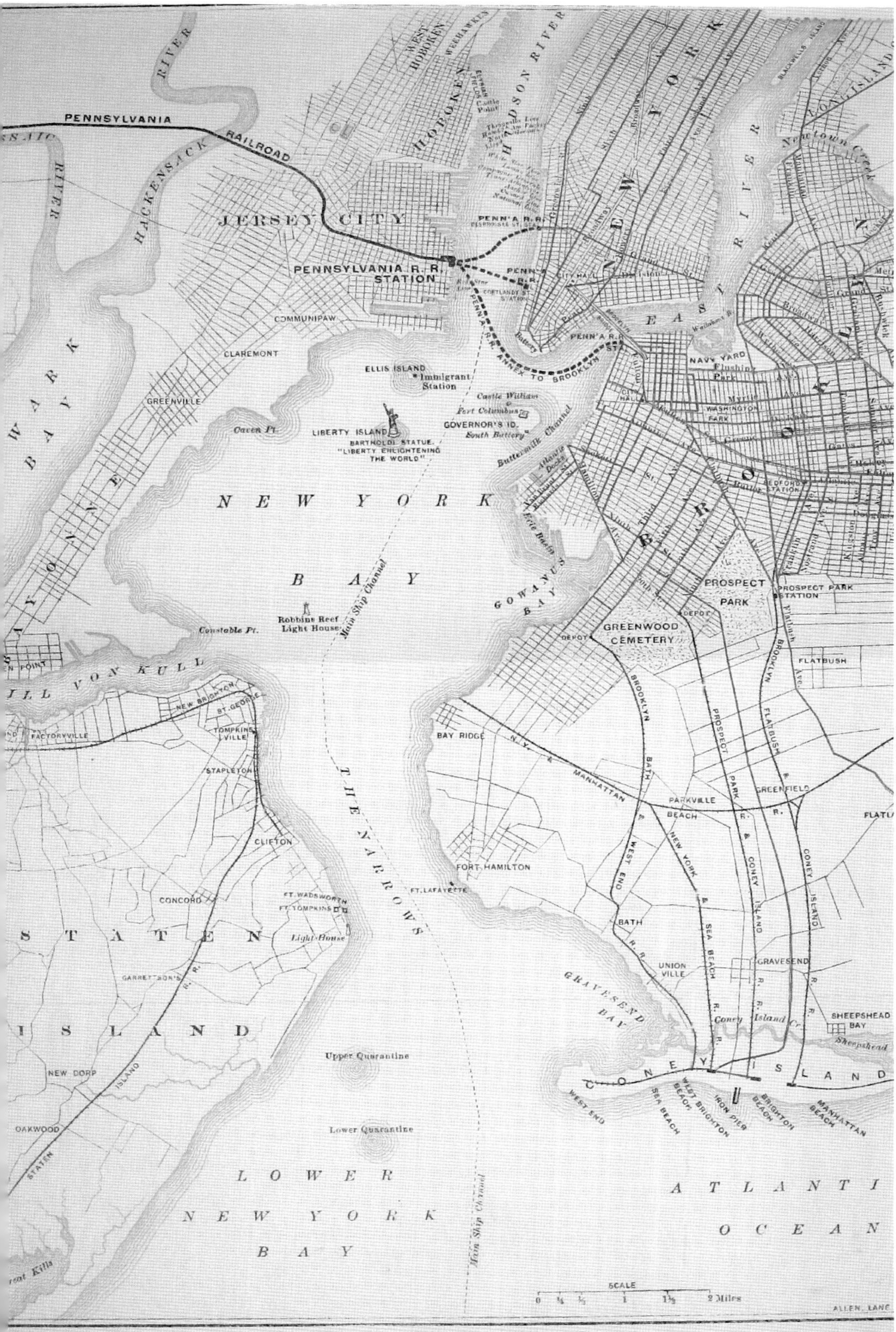

NEW YORK HARBOR.

PENNSYLVANIA RAILROAD

TO THE

COLUMBIAN EXPOSITION.

NEW YORK.

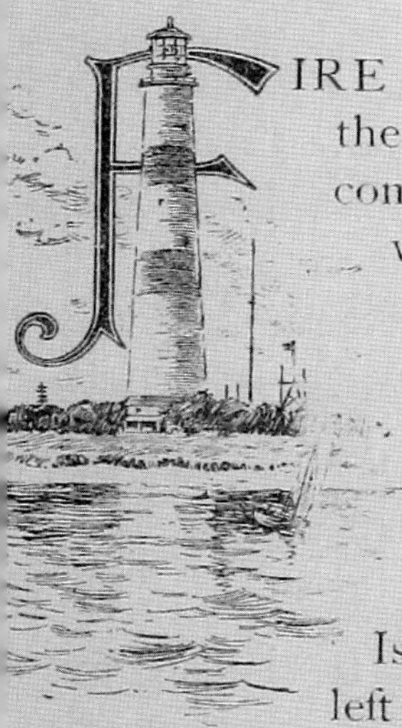

FIRE ISLAND Light has been sighted and passed; the twin lights on the highlands of Navesink have come into view, and now Sandy Hook, with its waste of sand, its light-house, and its embryotic fortifications is lying off to your left. Ahead of you is the quarantine ship, from which all vessels arriving from infected ports are boarded, and three miles beyond you can see the quarantine stations on Swinburne and Hoffman Islands. Now the shores of Long Island on your right and Staten Island on your left begin gradually to converge, and a few minutes later you find yourself within what is known as the Narrows, the passage-way from the outer vestibule, or lower bay, into the beautiful and capacious harbor of New York.

The health officer and the customs inspector have come aboard, and the latter is distributing blank forms upon which you are expected to make a statement of any dutiable goods that you may have among your luggage, the term dutiable applying to such articles as are not intended for your own personal use.

While this formality is being gone through with the harbor fortifications—Fort Wadsworth, Fort Hamilton, and Fort Lafayette—are left behind, the Narrows widen into New York Bay, and the Island of Manhattan, upon which is located the metropolis of America, lies directly in front of the steamer.

Bartholdi's colossal statue, "Liberty Enlightening the World," the largest statue ever constructed, rises to a height of something like three hundred feet above Liberty Island, which occupies an imposing position in the middle of the harbor, and you recall, as you gaze upon its gigantic proportions, that it was a gift of France to the United States to commemorate the good-will that has ever existed between the two nations. Through the mist that overhangs the water the East River Bridge, with its two sky-scraping towers and its sixteen hundred feet of space between—the largest suspension bridge in the world—looms up in the distance; Governor's Island, a most important feature in the harbor defense of New York, is now on your right, and Ellis Island, the landing-place for immigrants, has come into sight on your left, lying between Liberty Island and the New Jersey shore.

Now it is that you gather your first impressions of the chief city of the new world, the towering buildings, cupolas, and spires of which are before you. On the right is Brooklyn, the City of Churches, and on the left Jersey City, but between them lies the great pulsing heart of American civilization—New York.

Having landed, the choice of an hotel first engrosses your attention. The hotels of the city are numerous, and in point of location, rates, character of accommodations, and *cuisine* there is large variety. The more popular houses are located on upper Broadway and Fifth Avenue, and here you will discover a dozen or more from which you may choose, with a fair chance of being well satisfied. An excellent plan, when economy is an object, is

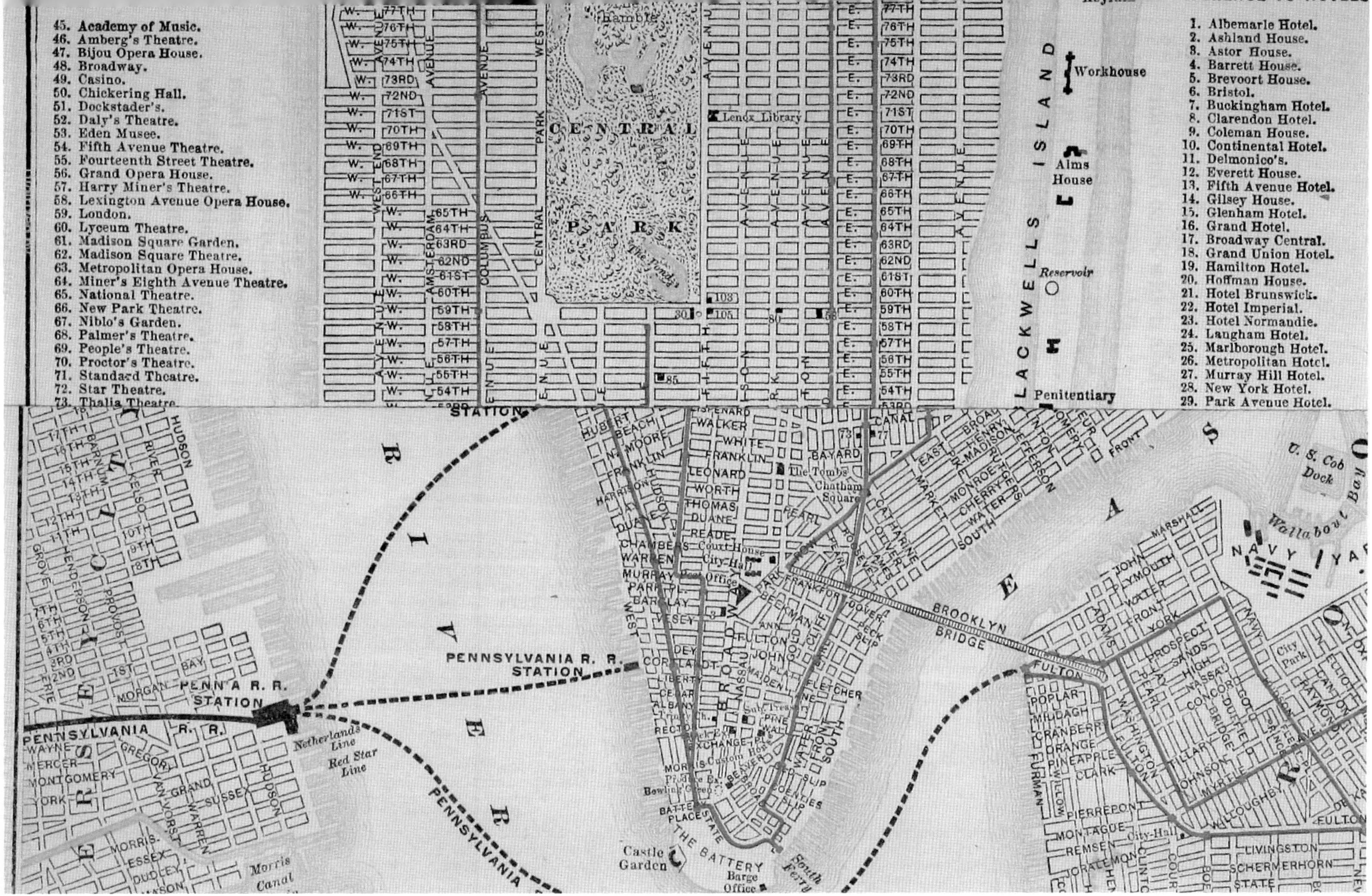
45. Academy of Music.
46. Amberg's Theatre.
47. Bijou Opera House.
48. Broadway.
49. Casino.
50. Chickering Hall.
51. Dockstader's.
52. Daly's Theatre.
53. Eden Musee.
54. Fifth Avenue Theatre.
55. Fourteenth Street Theatre.
56. Grand Opera House.
57. Harry Miner's Theatre.
58. Lexington Avenue Opera House.
59. London.
60. Lyceum Theatre.
61. Madison Square Garden.
62. Madison Square Theatre.
63. Metropolitan Opera House.
64. Miner's Eighth Avenue Theatre.
65. National Theatre.
66. New Park Theatre.
67. Niblo's Garden.
68. Palmer's Theatre.
69. People's Theatre.
70. Proctor's Theatre.
71. Standard Theatre.
72. Star Theatre.
73. Thalia Theatre.
1. Albemarle Hotel.
2. Ashland House.
3. Astor House.
4. Barrett House.
5. Brevoort House.
6. Bristol.
7. Buckingham Hotel.
8. Clarendon Hotel.
9. Coleman House.
10. Continental Hotel.
11. Delmonico's.
12. Everett House.
13. Fifth Avenue Hotel.
14. Gilsey House.
15. Glenham Hotel.
16. Grand Hotel.
17. Broadway Central.
18. Grand Union Hotel.
19. Hamilton Hotel.
20. Hoffman House.
21. Hotel Brunswick.
22. Hotel Imperial.
23. Hotel Normandie.
24. Langham Hotel.
25. Marlborough Hotel.
26. Metropolitan Hotel.
27. Murray Hill Hotel.
28. New York Hotel.
29. Park Avenue Hotel.
CENTRAL PARK
Lenox Library
BLACKWELLS ISLAND
Workhouse
Alms House
Reservoir
Penitentiary
BROOKLYN BRIDGE
PENNSYLVANIA R. R. STATION
PENN'A R. R. STATION
Netherlands Line
Red Star Line
Castle Garden
THE BATTERY
Barge Office
South Ferry
U. S. Cob Dock
Wallabout Bay
NAVY YARD
Morris Canal

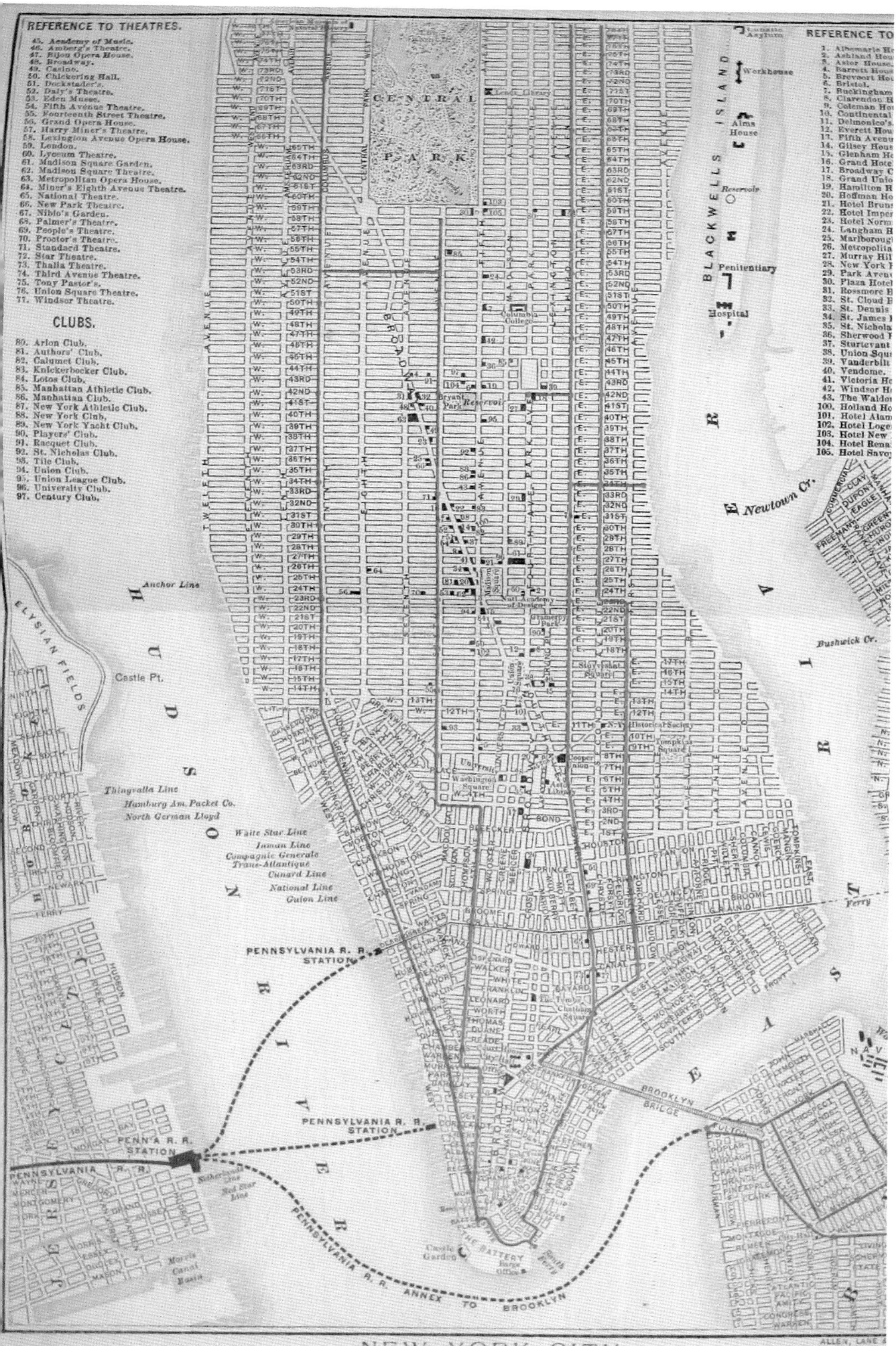

NEW YORK CITY.

to secure lodgings in a central location and patronize the restaurants and cafés which abound in the vicinity, and at many of which a *table d'hote* breakfast may be obtained for from twenty-five to fifty cents and a *table d'hote* dinner for from fifty cents to one dollar and fifty cents, usually with wine included.

The principal hotels are mentioned by name and located on the map of the city included in these pages.

Having settled upon a hotel you will now proceed to get a more definite knowledge of the city than you have hitherto acquired, and if you are wise you will walk at once to the nearest station of the Sixth Avenue branch of the Manhattan Elevated Railway. The chances are that it is not more than two or three blocks from your hotel. Mounting to the station for "down-town trains," on the west side of the street, you pay five cents for a ticket, which you deposit in a box at the entrance to the platform, and board the first train labeled "South Ferry" that comes along. In no better way than this can you get an idea of the people you have come among. The passengers in the car where you seat yourself are constantly changing. At each station some alight and others get on, and in your twenty minutes' ride the chances are you have had a glimpse of every type of New York resident. In this way, too, you are able to gather an impression from the car windows of several different and distinct sections of the city—the shopping district from Twenty-third Street to Fourteenth Street, the French quarter, and the old residence quarter, in the neighborhood of Washington Square, a glimpse of which, with its marble arch, may be had through some of the cross-streets over which you are whirled; the wholesale trade district, that lies just east of the long line of piers stretching along the North River; and then as the road approaches nearer to Broadway cheap stores, in front of which alluring bargain signs are hung to catch the unwary country visitor who must pass up this way from the ferry, grow marvelously frequent. The line, you find, comes to an end in Battery Park, at the southern extremity of the city, where the several branches of the elevated road join in a common station. Having descended to *terra firma* in front of an array of ferry-houses, from which boats connect with Brooklyn, Bay Ridge, Staten Island, and Ellis, Liberty, and Governor's Islands, you are in what was in the old colonial days the most fashionable part of the city. West of the ferries is the Barge Office, where the Surveyor of the Port has a branch office and the customs inspectors their headquarters, and where, during the interval between the abandonment of Castle Garden and the occupancy of Ellis Island, was the depot for the landing of immigrants. Here, too, is the United States Marine Hospital, and beyond, situated upon the fine sea wall which stretches around the lower edge of Battery Park, and from which a superb view of the harbor is obtainable, is the building known as Castle Garden, which has been in turn a fortification, a summer garden, and a landing depot for immigrants.

Bowling Green is only a few blocks away, but between the Battery and it, on Whitehall Street, are two structures worthy of notice—the United States Army building, where quartermasters' supplies and the like are stored, and the Produce Exchange, a magnificent edifice of granite, brick, terra cotta and iron, which cost three and a quarter millions of dollars, and on the floor of the main hall of which it is said seven thousand men could comfortably transact business at one time. An elevator will carry you to the top of the high tower, from which a bird's-eye view of the city can be obtained.

From Bowling Green you enter Broadway, the main artery of the metropolis, and a walk back to your hotel, a distance of about three miles, will not only afford you an excellent notion of the city, but give you a view of many points of interest as well.

In the next block, opposite the head of Wall Street, is Old Trinity Church, as fine an example of gothic architecture as is to be found in the city, and surrounded by a graveyard that is rich in historical interest, some of the headstones dating back to the time of the original church building, which was the first home of the Church of England in America. The church spire is two hundred and eighty-four feet high.

On Wall Street, the western end of which is at Trinity's door, are some of the principal office buildings of the city, an entrance to the Stock Exchange, the main fronts of which are on Broad and New Streets, the United States Sub-Treasury, and the Custom House. The scene within the Stock Exchange, the visitors' gallery of which is reached from Wall Street, will well repay a visit. From this building telegraph wires run to every part of the country and the financial pulse of the nation is taken at intervals of less than a second.

In the vaults of the Sub-Treasury, at the corner of Wall and Nassau Streets, are deposited millions of dollars of the nation's funds, but its interest does not lie so much in this fact as in the historic one that it occupies the site of old Federal Hall, on the balcony of which Washington took the oath of office as first President of the United States, in 1789. A bronze statue of Washington taking the oath adorns the steps of the present building.

Adjoining the Sub-Treasury is the United States Assay Office, erected in 1823, and the oldest building in the street, where bullion and old coin and plate of all descriptions are bought and melted into bricks to be used by the mints in coining.

The Custom House, a block nearer the river on the other side of the street, is a building of gray granite, in the doric style of architecture, with portico and high granite columns. As may be inferred from the fact that its average receipts in duties collected on imports is about $155,000,000 against less than $3,000,000 expenses, it is enormously profitable to the United States Government.

The principal building on Broadway between Wall Street and the Post-Office is that of the Equitable Life Assurance Society, on the east side of the thoroughfare, between Pine and Cedar Streets. Through it pass more than thirty thousand people daily, and it accommodates something like thirty-five hundred tenants. In its tower are the headquarters of the United States Signal Service in New York, on two of its upper floors is accommodated the Lawyer's Club, and on its ground floor and in the basement is the Cafe Savarin.

The Western Union Telegraph Company's building is a short distance above the Equitable, on the west side of Broadway, at the corner of Dey Street, an inspiring structure, in which are the headquarters of the telegraph company named. An idea of the company's business may be obtained from the statement that in 1890 it handled fifty-five million eight hundred and seventy-eight thousand seven hundred and sixty-two messages, and that its receipts were $22,387,027.91.

At the corner where Park Row on the east and Vesey Street on the west join Broadway are four buildings that merit your attention. The New York *Herald* building, of white marble, on your right, old St. Paul's Chapel across the way on your left—a chapel of Trinity parish and the only colonial relic among the churches of New York; the Astor House, at one time the principal hotel of the city, and still a good paying property. On the northeast corner of Broadway and Vesey Street, and directly ahead of you, filling up the triangle formed by Park Row on one side, Broadway on the other, and City Hall Park in the rear, the gray granite building of the United States Post-Office, with its dome modeled after that of the Louvre, pointing skyward on the Broadway side. The Post-Office building, in which the business done involves the handling on an average of over six hundred thousand letters daily and about nine thousand bags of newspaper mail, includes also the United States Courts, the

United States District Attorney's office, and offices used for other Federal purposes.

In the old colonial days City Hall Park, the last vestige of which you find north of the Post-Office, but which originally included the ground on which the Post-Office is built, was used for public celebrations, as five times a year a public bonfire was lighted upon it, and food and drink distributed at the expense of the town. It is now merely a beauty spot in the midst of a breathless field of business. Across its green the imposing newspaper structures of Park Row may be seen rising heavenward, while in the middle distance the city's municipal buildings give the scene a picturesqueness that is to be found nowhere else in the city. The City Hall, with its marble front and sides, and its cupola capped by a statue of justice, contains the offices of several city officials, including that of the Mayor. North of the City Hall is the New Court House, of white marble, while to the east is the old Hall of Records or Register's Office, a relic of the Revolutionary war.

Mercantile houses of more or less importance now crowd Broadway on both sides as you journey northward, and most of the places worth seeing are to be found off to the right. Leaving Broadway at Houston Street you will find only a few steps away on Mulberry Street, midway between Houston and Bleecker Streets, the headquarters of the New York police, and will learn that the force numbers about thirty-five hundred men, including one superintendent, four inspectors, and thirty-six captains.

A little further north another detour will be repaid by a view of the Astor Library, in Lafayette Place, a few doors south of Astor Place, which runs out of the main thoroughfare. This is a free reference library endowed by the Astor family, containing two hundred and sixty-eight thousand books and pamphlets, and possessing an estate valued at about $2,000,000. Near here is also the Cooper Union, founded by the famous American philanthropist, Peter Cooper, and including science and art schools for men and women and a free library. The Bible House, the home of the American Bible Society, which, since its institution in 1816, has distributed over fifty-three million Bibles, is situated directly opposite the Cooper Institute, in Astor Place, between Third and Fourth Avenues.

As you have walked north on Broadway you have noticed that your view has been obstructed at a certain point by a graceful church edifice of light-gray stone. This is Grace Church, and you find that it is adjoined by a parsonage and parish house of a similar style of architecture. Its congregation is among the wealthiest in New York.

A few blocks more and you come to Union Square, a park covering three and a half acres, which here breaks Broadway in two. It is ornamented, as are all the city squares and parks, with fountains, shrubbery, flowers, and statuary. From Union Square to Madison Square is a succession of retail houses, forming the other side of the shopping district which you saw from the elevated train in your ride southward. Broadway, north of Twenty-third Street, which is itself a great shopping thoroughfare, is given up for the most part to theatres, hotels, and apartment houses.

Having seen Broadway, or as much of it as is worth your while, it will be well for you to devote the rest of your day to Fifth Avenue. Entering upon it where it crosses Broadway and climbing Murray Hill, the fashionable residence quarter, you may continue your stroll to and into Central Park at Fifty-ninth Street. In this you will see the homes of the more important clubs, including the Reform, the Knickerbocker, the Calumet, the Manhattan, the New York, and the Union League. The Union Club and the Lotus are situated on Fifth Avenue, but south of Twenty-third Street, while the Manhattan Athletic Club and the New York Athletic Club are on side avenues, the former on Madison Avenue at Forty-fourth Street and the later on Sixth Avenue at Fifty-fifth Street. You will see, too, the mansions of many of New York's millionaires, including those of the Vanderbilts, between Fifty-first and Fifty-second Streets; and St. Patrick's Cathedral, the largest and handsomest church building in the United States.

A drive around Central Park and a visit to the Metropolitan Museum of Art situated therein should be considered necessary to obtain even a cursory impression of the city. The Park comprises eight hundred and forty acres, with nine miles of winding drives; its lakes and ponds cover an area of forty-three and one-quarter acres, and it includes among its features of interest an obelisk presented to the city by the Khedive of Egypt, and brought to this country from Alexandria in 1880. A menagerie, rich in animals of all kinds, takes up ten acres of the Park's land. The Metropolitan Museum of Art contains many valuable and famous pictures and some costly and rare collections of antiquities.

Thus far you have seen only the bright side of New York. A visit to the Bowery, to Chinatown, and to the Italian quarter, where may be seen the dark side, cannot fail to interest you if you are a student of human nature; and if, moreover, you care to note how a city grows it may be well to take trips on the elevated roads to their northern *termini*, when you will be able to form some conception of how New York's million and a half of souls are housed, and how more room is being made each year for a constantly increasing population.

Having seen New York, whether well or ill depends upon the time you have devoted to it, you make ready for your nine hundred mile journey across the continent to Chicago and the Columbian Exposition. The Pennsylvania Railroad's line you learn is the safest, the speediest, the most comfortable, and the most picturesque, and you choose it, as a matter of course. The company has two passenger stations in New York, one at the foot of Desbrosses Street for the accommodation of passengers like yourself from up-town, and one at the foot of Cortlandt Street for the convenience of business men and others who are engaged in the lower part of the city. A cab will carry you from your hotel to Desbrosses Street Ferry in from fifteen to thirty minutes, and the cabman will expect a dollar for doing so. If you have a half hour to spare the Sixth Avenue elevated road to Grand Street and from there a cross-town car to the ferry will be a cheaper route; or you may continue on the elevated train to Cortlandt Street, from which station the down-town ferry is but about three minutes' walk distant. You will find the ferry-houses roomy and comfortable, while as for the ferry-boats that carry you across the North or Hudson River to Jersey City, the eastern terminus of the Pennsylvania Railroad, they are veritable floating palaces, large, light, and luxuriously appointed, with an upper saloon and deck from which a most excellent view of the river front and shipping of the city may be had.

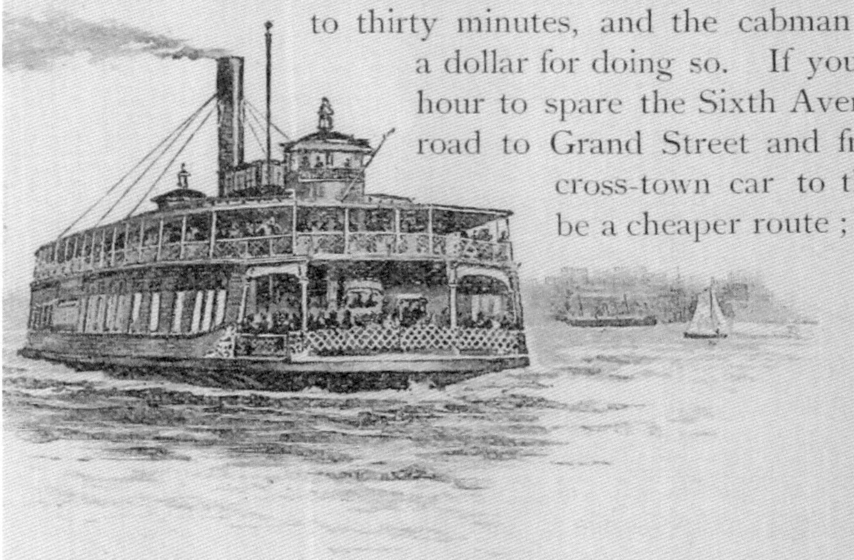

THE START FOR THE WEST.

A GREAT high, wide-spreading, graceful arch, through the white glass of which the sunlight filters down over lines of long, sleek passenger cars, made up into trains about to start for various sections of the country. A half dozen surcharged locomotives far away down the vast transparent roofed inclosure are sending up clouds of white steam, the music of which, as it comes moaning from the open safety valves, mingles with the clatter of hurrying baggage trucks, the distant rattle of whirling ratchet wheels making fast an arriving ferry-boat, the sonorous voices of the conductors in blue uniforms and silver buttons standing at the head of the long lanes of platforms and directing passengers to their soon-to-be-moving trains, and the incessant drone of the overladen newsboys with their daily and weekly papers, the latest magazines, the newest novels, and the inevitable silk traveling caps.

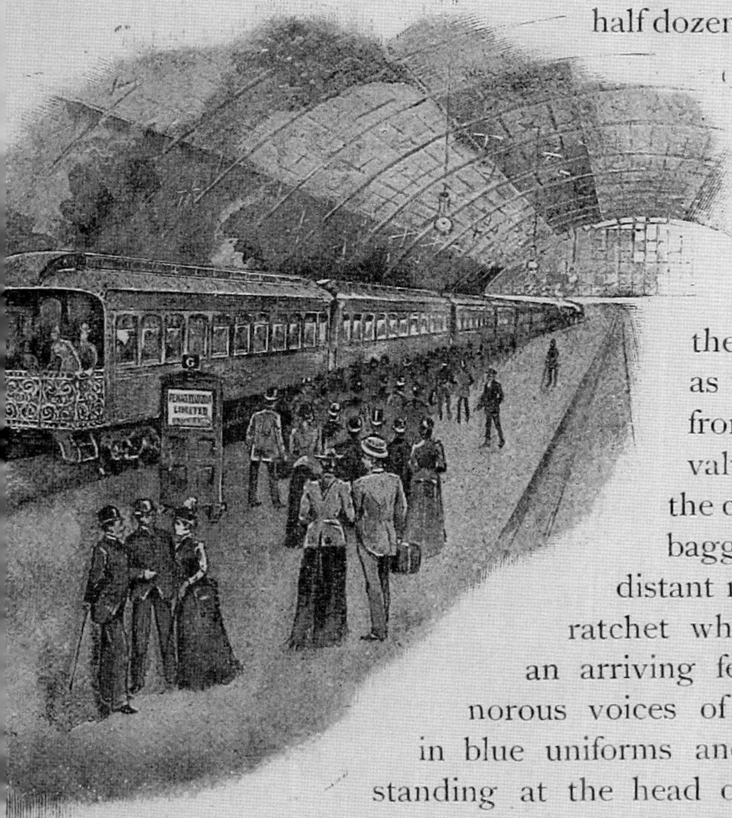

You are in the Jersey City station of America's greatest railroad—the Pennsylvania. Behind you, across the river, lies the metropolis of the new world—New York; before you, at the end of nine hundred miles of glistening steel rails, rises the eighth wonder of the world, the city that was built in a day—Chicago. A clock above your head tells you that it is ten minutes after ten in the morning, and a time-table in your hand informs you that before this hour to-morrow you will have arrived at your Mecca, the Exposition that celebrates four centuries of American development.

"Philadelphia, Pittsburg, Chicago, and the West!"

The voice of the conductor of the most sumptuous railway train that the mind of man ever conceived—the Pennsylvania Limited—rings out clear and sharp above the babel of other sounds. A negro porter takes your portmanteau and your rugs, and you hurry forward. Your ticket indicates your location for the journey. It is in "Car 2," perhaps, "Lower 12," which means the middle Pullman sleeping car of the train, and one of the lower berths at the rear end; or it is possible that you have secured the drawing-room in this car, which will afford you greater privacy, though for that matter a section, including an upper and a lower berth, will be all that you require should you merely wish a compartment to yourself. Here in "Lower 12," for instance, the upper berth not having been sold, you find that you are quite alone, and that if you feel so inclined you may draw the richly embossed velvet curtains which are draped from a brass rod above and shut yourself away from the eyes of your fellow-passengers.

Scarcely have you begun to marvel over the luxury of your surroundings than, glancing out of the window, you realize that the train is moving. So gradually, so smoothly have the wheels started upon their twenty-four hours of revolution that you have not had the slightest indication until this moment that you have passed from under that mammoth roof-span—the greatest in the

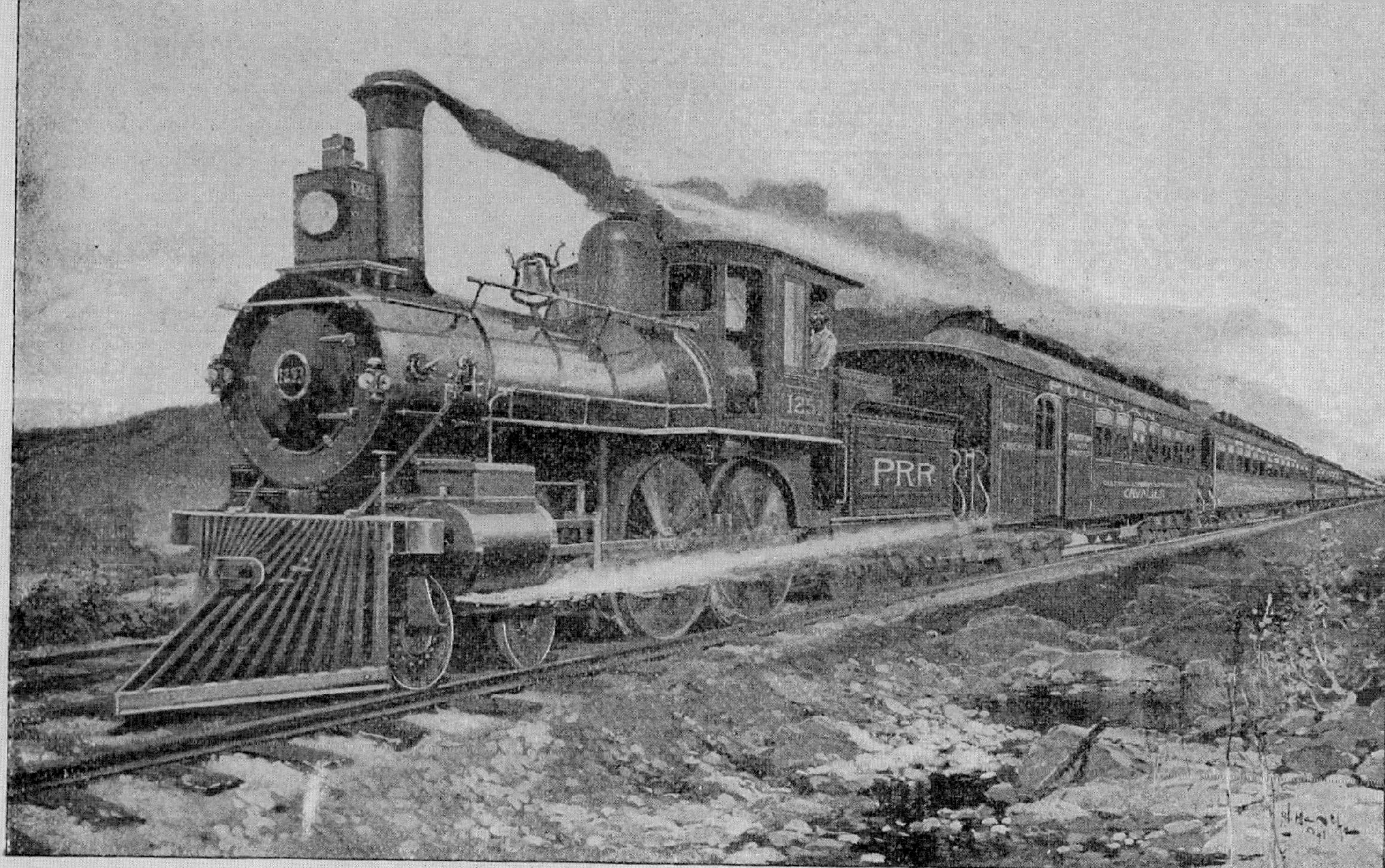

"PENNSYLVANIA LIMITED" AT TOP SPEED.

world—and have glided out upon the elevated road-bed that carries the tracks of the Pennsylvania Railroad Company over the streets of Jersey City and out into the broad stretch of meadows beyond.

The day is very fair. The morning sunshine stealing in between the silken window draperies transforms the rich browns of the upholstery into a glorious symphony in gold. The brass work, brightly polished, glistens in the warm rays, and the delicate tints of the ceiling decoration glowing in the light admitted by the double line of ventilators, join in the general harmony of color, which is reflected again and again by a score or more of dainty mirrors. You have been told that you may breakfast on the train, and you wonder where. At this moment the negro porter looms up in the distance, and the man who occupies the compartment opposite

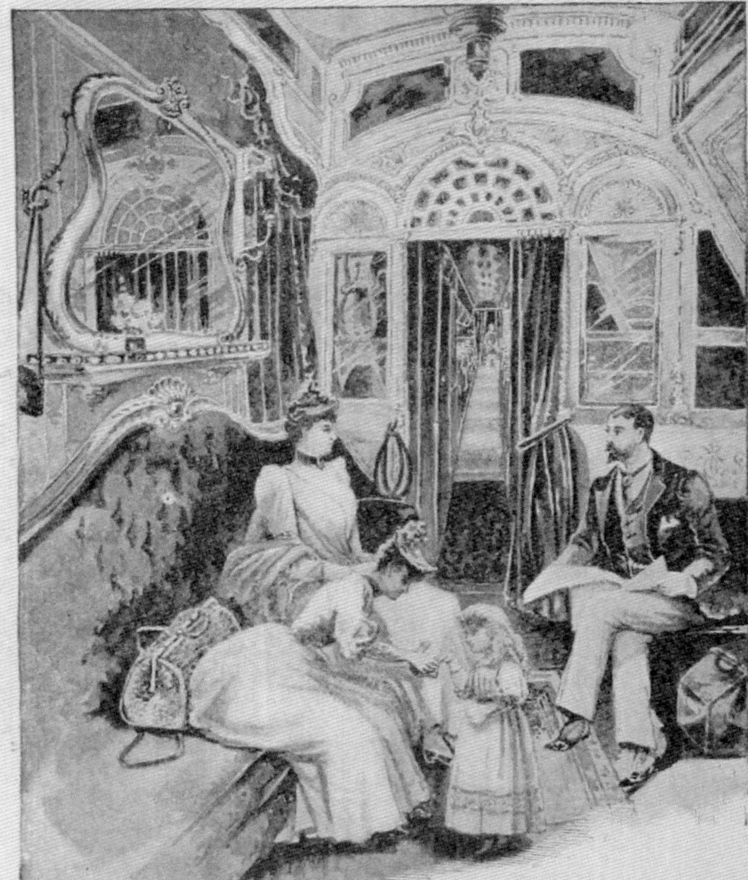

A DRAWING-ROOM.

to you, you notice, touches a button conveniently placed in the wall between the windows, and a bell tinkles somewhere far away. You note that the porter disappears for an instant, only to reappear ; he has glanced at the electrical indicator in the brief interim, and now he has come straight to your neighbor and is awaiting his commands. You seize the opportunity to inquire about your breakfast, and learn that you can be served in the dining car, which is two cars forward.

The inclosed passage-way through which you pass from one car to another is the vestibule feature of the train, and you can readily realize that not only does it afford entire safety to passengers, who in the old days were warned against going from car to car while trains were in motion, but that it aids very materially in preventing that disagreeable rocking from side to side which is inevitable without it. The vestibule, too, with its strong steel framework is a most effective safeguard against telescoping, and as you pass on this discovery gives to you a sense of security which you do not fail to appreciate.

The car which is between yours and the dining car is similar in every way to your own ; but as you walk through it you observe another feature of the train which up to this time has escaped you. A mulatto girl in a blue serge frock, white apron, and white cap is arranging a pillow for an elderly lady, who is evidently an invalid, upon a couch in the drawing-room, the door of which stands open, revealing an apartment as cosy, comfortable, and beautiful as any bijou boudoir in the land. The mulatto girl, the conductor tells you, is the train's ladies' maid, and is at the service of all of the women passengers.

There is a sparkle of delicate glassware and polished silver, reflecting snowy linen ; a glint of china, frail and transparent as an egg shell ; a breath of fresh flowers, and a musical clicking of knives and forks. White-coated and aproned waiters move to and fro with deftly balanced trays of smoking viands, and when

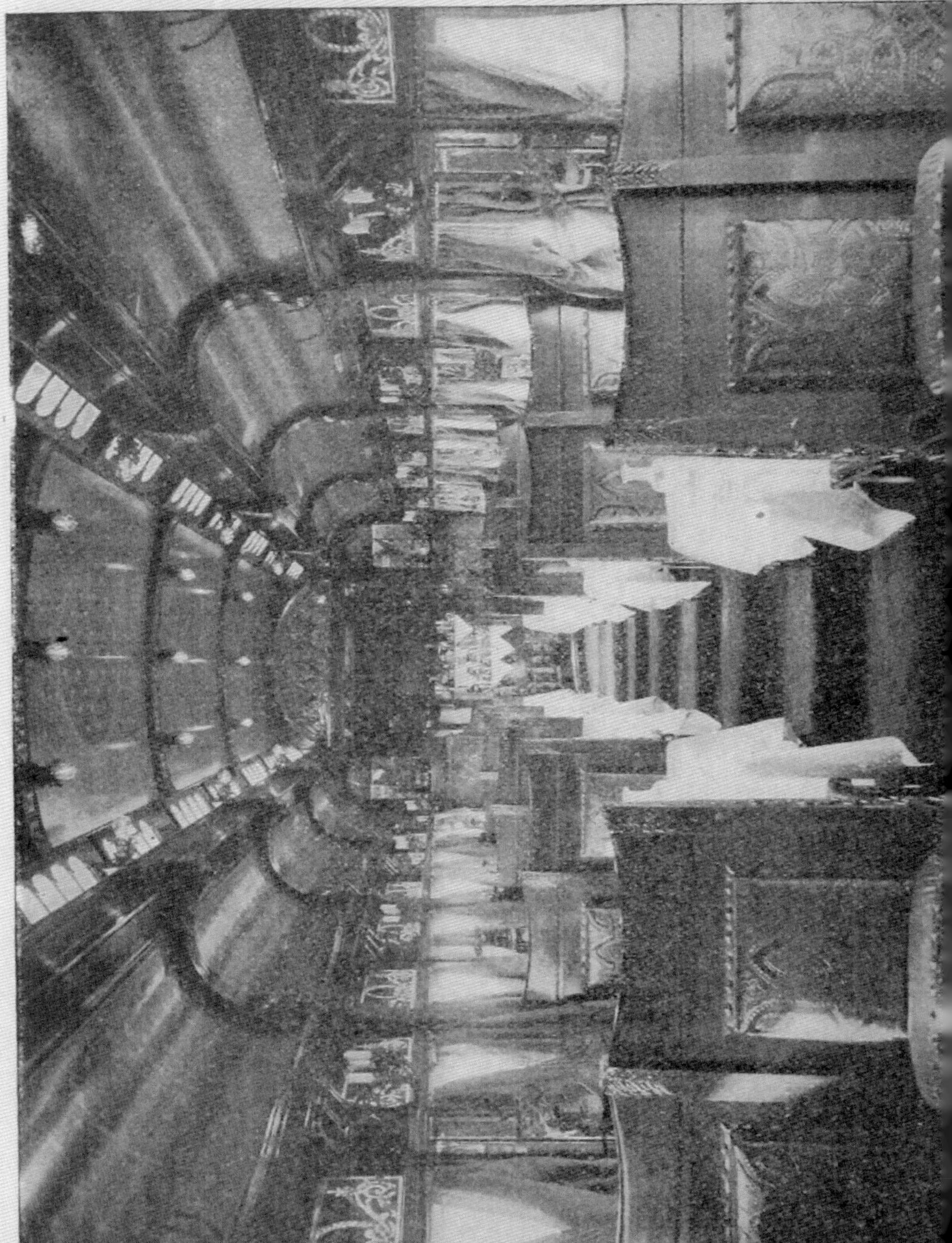

a blue-uniformed officer, the conductor of the dining car, has ushered you to a seat, one of these waiters places a napkin and a menu before you. You give your order, and while it is being cooked in the kitchen which occupies a third or more of the car, but which is dexterously hidden from sight, as you sit facing it, by a sideboard on which there is a dazzling array of plate and glassware, you may indulge in whatever fruit the season affords, glancing now and then out of the broad windows at the country through which the train is gliding at a speed which, so easily does it move, you cannot begin to realize.

Already you have crossed the meadows where are situated the railroad company's repair shops, freight buildings, and coaling platforms; you have crossed the Passaic River four miles from where it empties into Newark Bay, and are whirling through the city of Newark itself, the first city in point of population and wealth in New Jersey.

Before Elizabeth is reached you have your breakfast before you, but you stop eating for a moment to look at what was the first English settlement in the State, and what is now one of the chief suburban residence places of New York. Rahway, another manufacturing town, flashes by, and then, just as you have finished eating, and are thinking about an after-breakfast cigar, the Raritan River glimmers beneath you, and the train dashes into New Brunswick and out again, giving you just a peep at the stately old buildings and verdant campus of Rutgers College, which was chartered by King George III., of England, in 1770—Queen's College then, of course—and of several mills and factories, the roofs of which are on a level with the car windows.

"Smoking car, sir! Yes, sir! Next car forward, sir!"

If you were suddenly set down in your own club you could not be more snugly ensconced than you are in this warm-colored room, with its low, softly-cushioned wicker chairs, its velvet

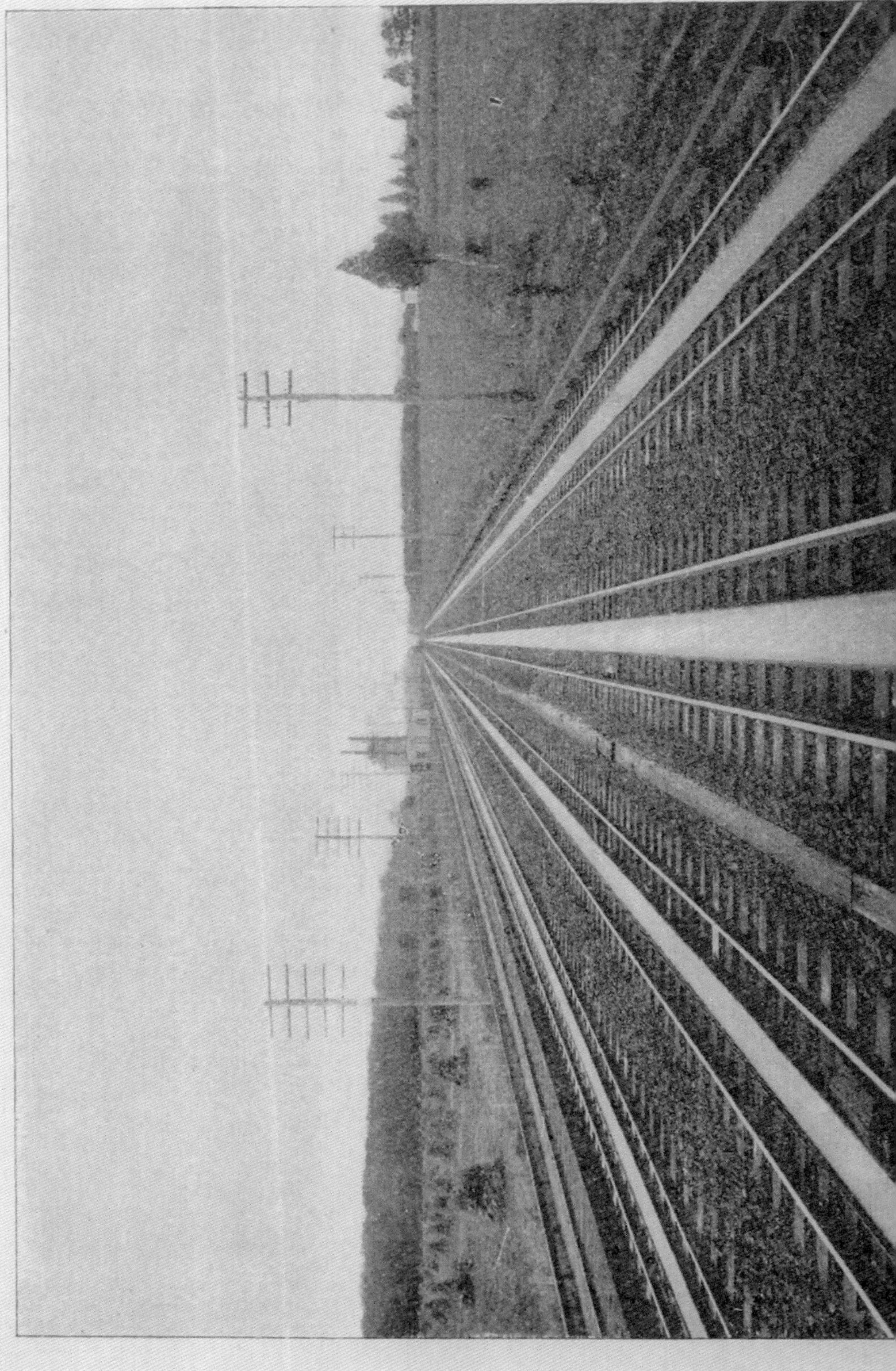

couch, its writing-desks, its book-cases, and its square tables laden with the morning newspapers and the current periodical literature. Beyond the curtained doorway yonder is the buffet, with which you can communicate by means of an electric button always at hand, and from which you can procure whatever you may desire in the way of liquid refreshment or cigars. Beyond this is the barber shop, from which entrance is had to the bath-room, and still further forward is the baggage-room, where your trunks, checked at your hotel in New York, are being carried along with you, not to be seen again until you find them at the Chicago hotel of your choice.

The train is now making good time through a generally level country, watered by streams that flow between picturesquely wooded banks, and cultivated by well-to-do, energetic farmers, who send their produce to both New York and Philadelphia. As the smoke of your cigar curls from your lips and clouds for an instant the broad window pane you catch a glimpse of a station flying by on your right. It is Princeton Junction, and the smoothly-shaven man with glasses who sits near to you, and who glances out across the fields with a half-regretful smile upon his face, will tell you, if you ask him, that three miles away, at the top of yonder ridge, is Princeton College, his *alma mater.* Princeton College, he will inform you, is "one of the foremost institutions of learning in the country, and from it have graduated many of America's brightest minds." About old Nassau Hall, the main college edifice, clings many historical reminiscences. During the Revolutionary war it was occupied alternately as a barrack and a hospital by both the British and American forces, and it bears to this day the marks made upon its walls by cannon balls during the battle of Princeton, in 1777.

The Trenton of to-day is noted principally for its potteries, some of the finest art ware manufactured in the United States being the product of its skilled artisans.

The Delaware River is crossed in a flash, and you have passed into the rich farming and grazing country of Bucks County in Pennsylvania. Fifty-eight miles have now been traversed, and a few minutes later you are among what may be considered the suburbs of Philadelphia; Bristol and a succession of smaller villages lying along the west bank of the Delaware containing many residences of Philadelphia business men, who make the journey to and from that city daily. Now you begin to notice mammoth manufactories, from the tall chimneys of which the smoke is pouring, and row after row of small brick houses with white shutters and low, white door-steps, and you know by this sign that you are in the outlying districts of the city of the Quakers. Street after street you cross at an elevation above grade, and then you are once more plunged suddenly into sylvan scenes of the most picturesque description. Fairmount Park, with its macadamized drives, its hills, and its dales, rises above you and then sweeps away to the silver Schuylkill at your feet. Oft

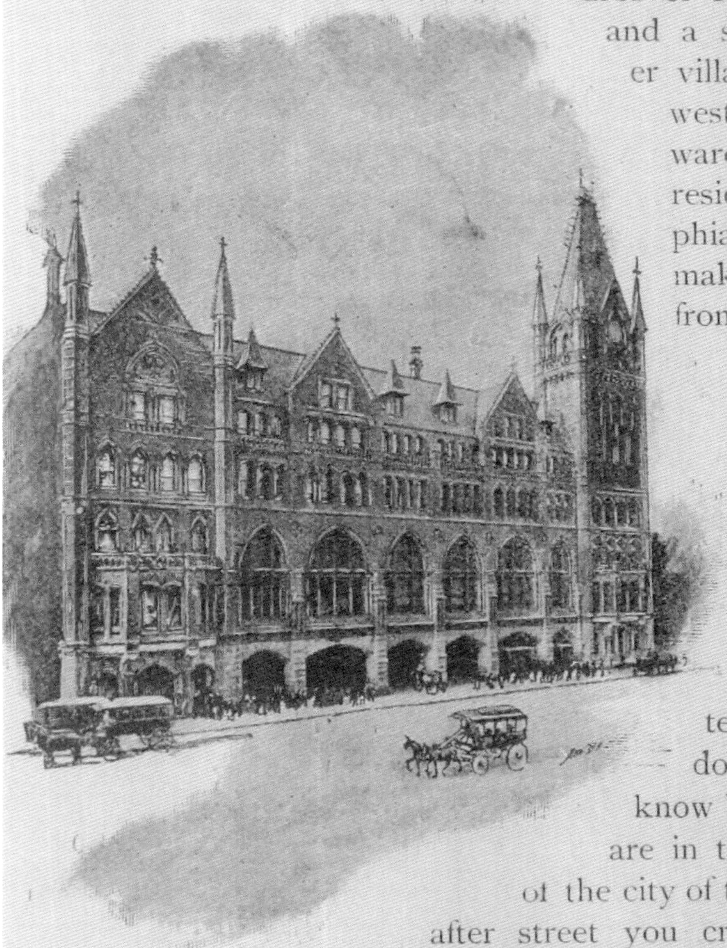

BROAD STREET STATION, PHILADELPHIA.

to your right, rising above the rich foliage, you see, as the train thunders over the bridge which spans the river, the surviving relics of the World's Fair of 1876—the white-domed Memorial Hall, which served as an art gallery, and the lower, conservatory-like building, that was then, and has been ever since, devoted to a horticultural display. The city's zoological gardens are on your left as your train sweeps around a long curve prior to recrossing the river at a point farther south, and gliding into the city proper over an elevated road similar to that over which you were carried out of Jersey City.

The magnificent scenery in which the Pennsylvania's route to Chicago is so rich lies for the most part west of Philadelphia. The journey has now really just been commenced, and after a brief stop at the Broad Street Station, during which you notice that the latest stock and produce quotations have been received and posted on a convenient bulletin-board in this cosiest of smoking-rooms, you walk through the train to the observation car, which is attached to the rear end.

If you have been pleasantly astonished at the elegant and complete comfort of the smoking car and its accessories you are sure to be equally amazed at the delicious luxury of the car which is designed primarily for the women passengers, but which is as much yours as theirs. The rattan furniture, upholstered in rich velvets, the soft carpets, the wide and high windows, slightly bowed, with their sumptuous draperies, the writing-desks, and tables, and book-shelves, similar to those you have just left in the smoker, are but incidents. The chief feature of the car lies beyond these in the extreme rear. At first glance it reminds you of a piazza upon which this beautiful room opens out, and a piazza from which the view is constantly changing. It is as broad as the car and equally as deep. There is room upon it for a dozen or more chairs. Its sides are protected by the car's sides, which extend out to meet the ornate brass railing that incloses its end, and the car's roof is its canopy. As the train glides out once more into the open country, through a landscape that is probably more like an English landscape than anything to be found elsewhere on the American continent, you notice on either hand the picturesque villas and manor houses of many of Philadelphia's wealthiest citizens, who here make their home the year round; but from your present position you notice something else as well. The road-bed, with its four tracks, stretching away behind this fast-flying hotel of yours, is, you see, in the most perfect order. Its heavy steel rails, polished bright as mirrors, rest upon evenly-spaced cross-ties, imbedded in evenly-broken stone ballast.

You notice, too, that your train is protected by the block signal system, and that no other train is permitted in the block between telegraph stations on which you are running until you have passed out of it and into the next beyond, and you are thus assured that to be overtaken and run into by a train which follows is a simple impossibility.

"A wonderful road," remarks your next neighbor; "the only road in America which combines the three essentials of perfect travel—*safety*, *speed*, and *comfort*. The company not only employs these block signals, which you must have observed, but the interlocking switch, which is another safeguard, and the air-brake, which, you know, places the speed of the train entirely in the hands of the engineman, who, from his position in the cab of the locomotive, is best fitted to look after it. In fact, not a single point has been overlooked by the Pennsylvania Railroad Company in securing to its patrons absolute safety. Accidents to its passenger trains are almost unknown.

"In the matter of speed," your neighbor continues, "the company is constantly making improvements. Years ago it introduced these track tanks," and as he speaks you see beneath you, between the tracks over which you are flying, a long, narrow pan of water. "The locomotive," he goes on, "takes up water from

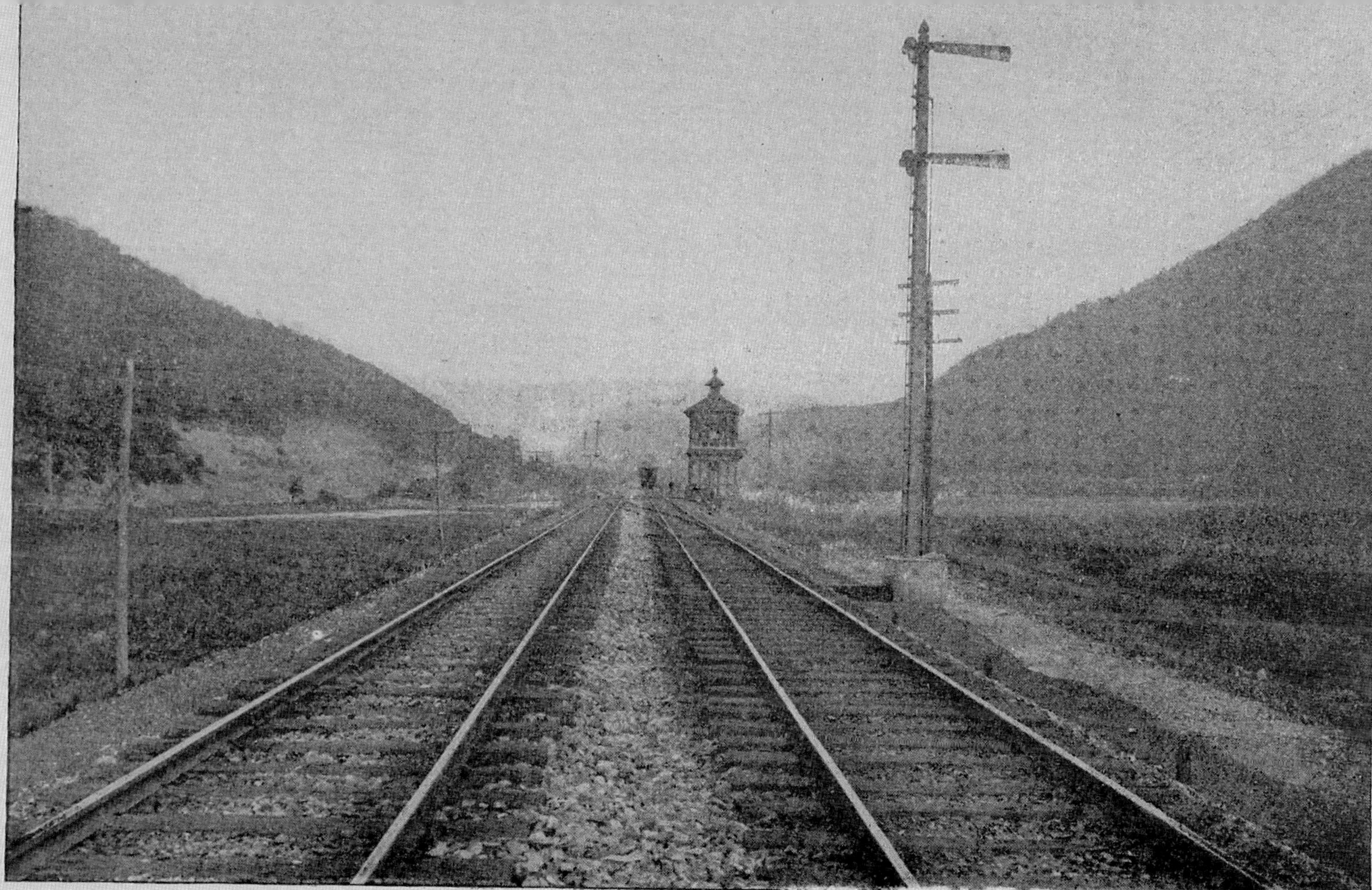

PENNSYLVANIA RAILROAD BLOCK SIGNAL TOWER.

these as it goes, without materially slacking speed. The heavy rails and the perfect road-bed are other adjuncts valuable in this direction ; as are also the company's stone bridges. Of late the line of road, too, has been very considerably straightened. Curves have been taken out and heavy grades lessened. The Pennsylvania, you see, considers speed an essential, but always secondary to safety. As for the comfort it secures its patrons I need not speak. The train you are on now is without a peer on the globe. You have here not merely comfort, but luxury. In no hotel in the country can you find more conveniences.''

The idea strikes you, possibly, that you would like to write a letter to catch to-morrow morning's European mail. You had not time before leaving, perhaps. You would like to write, you say, but you fear the motion of the car, gentle and almost imperceptible as it is, would make your chirography totally indecipherable.

Your neighbor smiles and asks you if you failed to notice the young man seated before a desk in the little compartment at the other end of this car. And then you learn that he is a stenographer and typewriter, and that what you dictate he will put into plainly printed characters for you, and that he will post it at the next stopping-place, whence it will go by fast mail back to New York, and leave to-morrow morning on the outgoing steamer.

Shortly after this the conductor of the dining car announces that luncheon is being served, and if your appetite is equal to a dozen iced blue points, a cup of bouillon, a chop or cutlet, and a salad, with an ice and *café noir*, you may gratify it.

Meanwhile you have passed through Delaware and Chester Counties in Pennsylvania, with their suburban homes and hotels, and before your luncheon is fairly under way you are speeding across Lancaster County, which comprises some of the most fertile farming land and the best kept farms in the State. The general surface of this county is an undulating plain, broken by a few

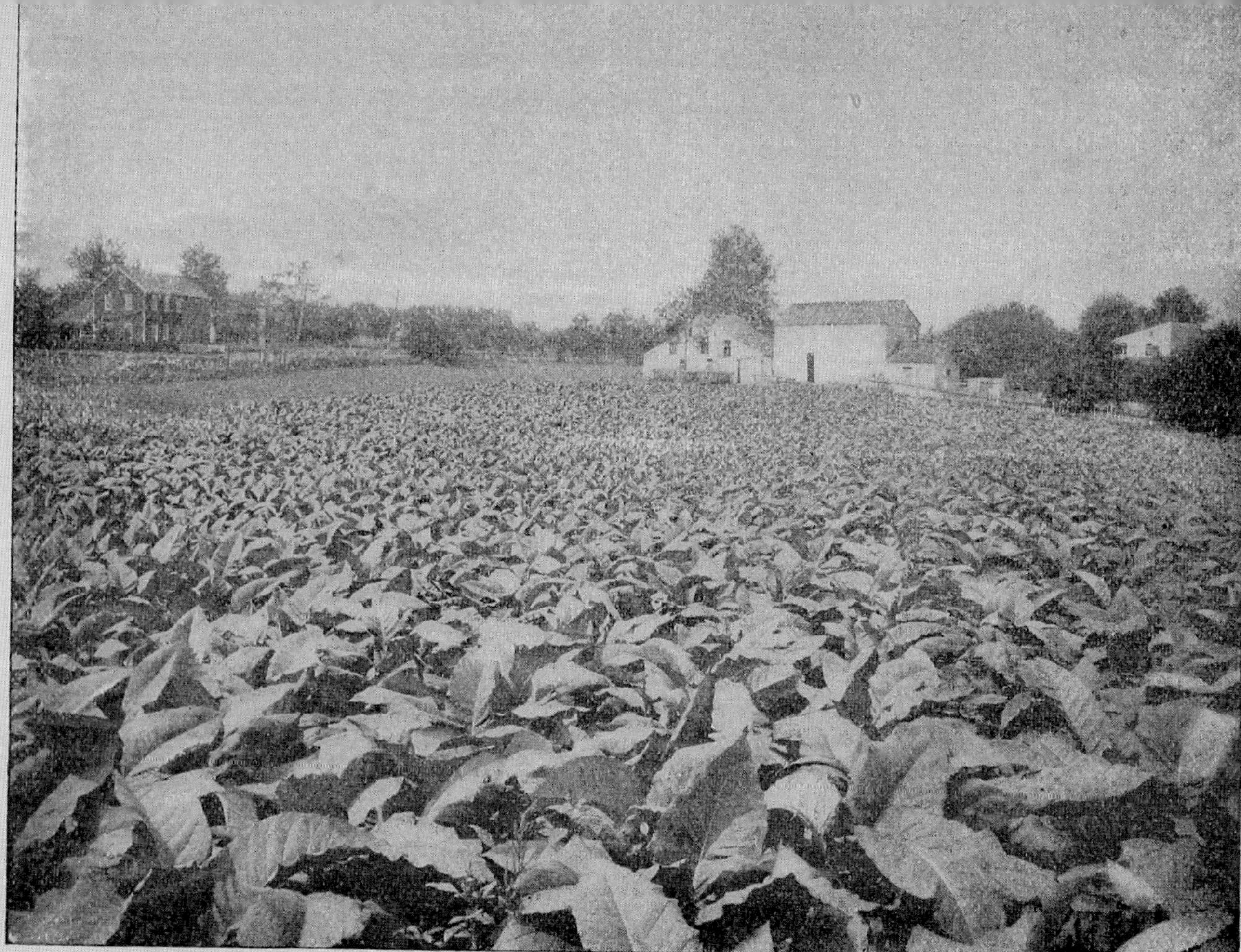

A LANCASTER COUNTY, PENNSYLVANIA, TOBACCO FIELD.

abrupt elevations, and the picture presented to your view from the car window is for the most part one of vari-colored patches, produced by the well-cultivated fields. Here you may notice the tobacco plant growing in rank abundance, for the cultivation and manufacture of this weed into cigars is one of Lancaster County's chief sources of revenue. The city of Lancaster, where Robert Fulton, the inventor of the steamboat, was reared and educated, looms up to your right, but the line of road only skirts it, and a glimpse of its church spires and the chimneys of its cotton mills and breweries is all that you are afforded.

Presently the Susquehanna River is discovered on your left, flowing placidly between low-lying banks, and just as the hands of your watch approach the hour of three the train rolls smoothly into the station at Harrisburg, the capital of the Keystone State. To the north is the Lebanon Valley, embracing an enormous area of highly-cultivated territory, abounding in iron ore and dotted with manufactories, while to the south lies the Cumberland Valley, second to no region in America of the same extent in picturesqueness, fertility, and mineral wealth, and including one of the show places of the United States, the Battlefield of Gettysburg, where, in 1863, took place the most stirring and momentous engagement of the war between the North and the South.

Once out of the Harrisburg Station and on the road again you have spread out before you an uninterrupted perspective of sparkling waters, verdant islands, rolling hills, and sloping woodland.

Five miles farther on and you have reached the Kittatinny Mountains, the first of the great Allegheny range, and bending abruptly to the west your train thunders over the Susquehanna River on a bridge thirty-six hundred and seventy feet in length. To your right rise gigantic ridges sundered by the waters in their passage, but leaving numerous rocks in the channel to break the river into rapids and fret it into foam, while to your left the stream sweeps away, with its wooded islands, towards Harrisburg, which you have left behind, but the steeples and domes of which are still in view.

You have sought the observation car again, and the pictures that are presented to your view in rapid succession are alternately

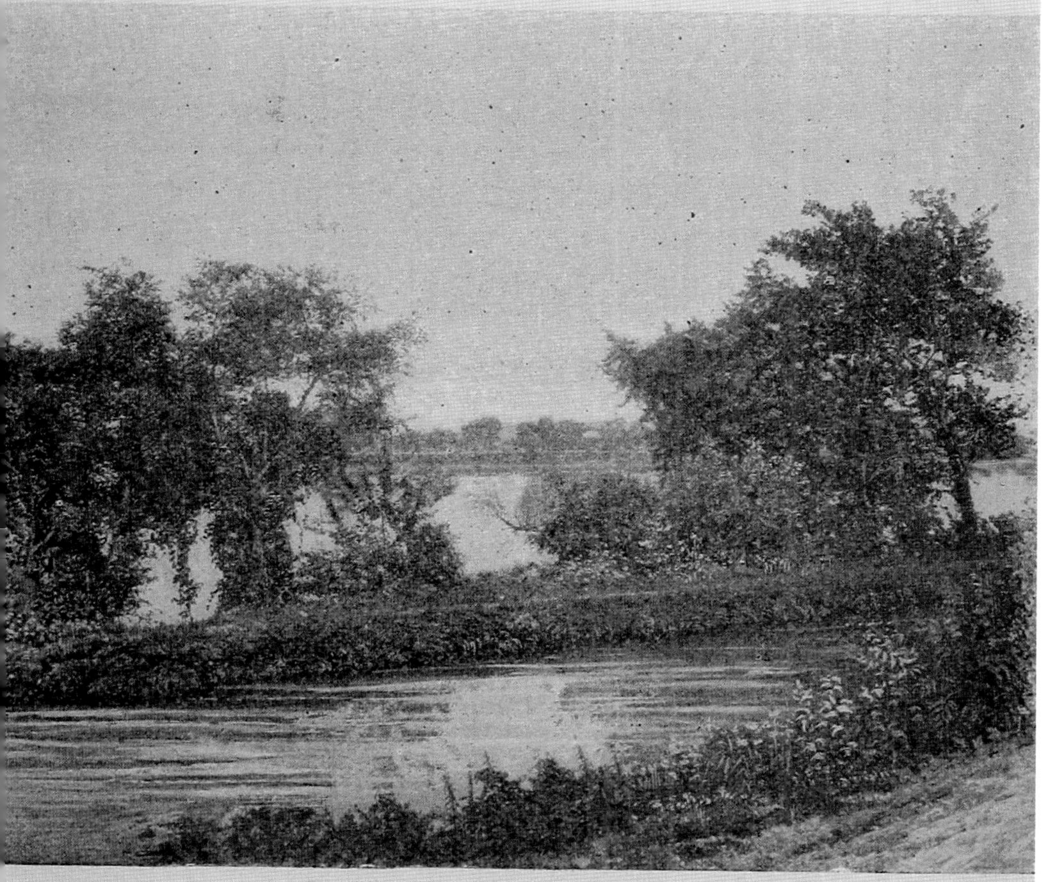

BY RIVER AND CANAL.

nagnificent in their wild grandeur and poetically idyllic in their juiet beauty. Leaving the Susquehanna, the road now follows he beautiful blue Juniata in its course through the mountains and alleys, until its sources are reached amid the great Alleghenies. The miniature river, picking a path for itself through the outlying mountains, has apparently overcome the obstacles in its way by strategy as well as power. At many places it has dashed boldly against the wall before it and torn it asunder, while at others you find it tortuously winding around the obstruction and creeping stealthily through secret valleys and secluded glens. So your train, flying along by its side, now passes through broad, cultivated valleys, and a moment later plunges into a ravine so narrow that the road-bed is but a ledge of overhanging rock. Here a mountain spur is tunneled through, and farther on, so tortuous becomes the stream, that you find yourself crossing and recrossing it in your flight westward.

Mifflin, with its memories of Indian wars ; Lewistown, near the site of which once dwelt the famous Mingo chief, Logan ; Mount Union, at the entrance to Jack's Narrows, a wild and rugged gorge ; Mill Creek and its sand quarries ; Huntingdon and Tyrone are passed in turn, and now you are approaching Altoona, where are located the celebrated shops of the Pennsylvania Railroad Company. Your ride in the open air has given you an appetite that demands satisfaction, but the knowledge that just the other side of Altoona you will pass through some of the grandest mountain scenery on the route induces you to keep your seat, and for keeping it you are amply repaid.

A brief stop is made at the Altoona Station, and then, with all steam on, the giant locomotive at the head of your train begins the ascent of the heaviest grade on the line. The valley beside you sinks lower and lower, until it becomes a vast gorge, the bottom of which is hidden by impenetrable gloom. Far in the depths cottages appear for a moment, only to disappear in the darkness, and then, just as night is falling, you begin the circuit of the world-famous Horse-shoe Curve, the most stupendous piece of engineering ever accomplished ; the wonder and admiration of travelers from the four corners of the globe ; the one feature of American railroad construction that you have been told required the utmost courage to attempt and the most miraculous skill to achieve. And now, as the enormous bend, sweeping first north, then curving westward, and still curving away to the south again, presents itself to your view, you confess that you did not begin to estimate its grandeur. An eagle soars majestically away from some crag above your head and floats with extended wings over the gulch that makes your brain reel as you glance downward, so

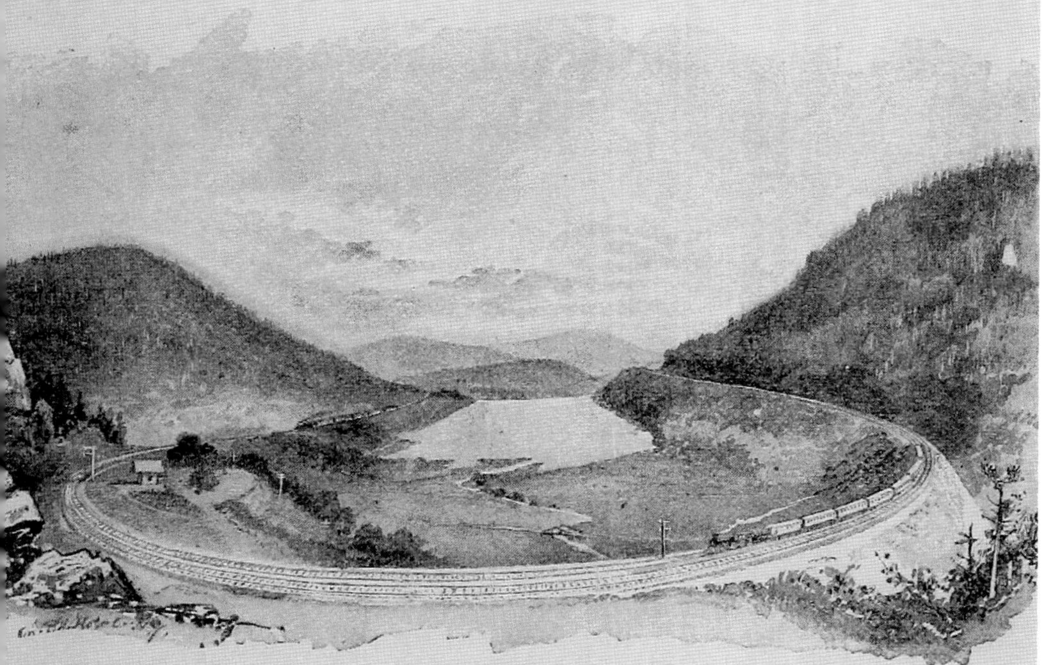

HORSE-SHOE CURVE.

deep is it. The clouds into which you are climbing bend low and hide the rugged top of the mountain to whose beetling side you are clinging, forming a whitish gray canopy that extends half way across the dizzy chasm. It is all so large, so grand, so majestic, that you admit that your imagination has been unequal to the task of picturing it.

Your train is dwarfed by its surroundings until it seems but a mere toy moving at snail's pace around this tremendous loop of shining metal threads. Across the chasm another train, whose lights, as it glides through the shadow, give it the semblance of a flight of fire-flies, appears to be racing with your own. In reality it is approaching you, and as you whirl around the northern end of the horse-shoe at the head of the valley, it goes thundering by, and a new race begins with an exchange of sides.

The clouds which have dipped into the gorge roll majestically away at this moment, and far below you, trailing in and out, you descry a tiny stream of water, the winding course of which is suddenly lost to sight among the mountains which bar your view. It is a tributary of the Juniata, and its waters eventually find their way into Chesapeake Bay; while across the mountain, along whose rugged breast you are now climbing in search of an opening westward, babbles another rivulet that empties itself into the Conemaugh, and thus from river to river until it reaches the mighty Mississippi, and finally the Gulf of Mexico. In a word, you are about to cross the great dividing range of the continent, and at a height of something like two thousand feet above the level of the Atlantic.

At Allegrippus the grandeur of the mountains seems to culminate. Gazing to the east, range after range rises into view, each fainter of outline than the other, until the last fades into the azure of the horizon. Now the valleys begin gradually to rise again, the mountains sink down, and you find yourself upon what appears to be a rugged plain where industry has found a place for furnaces, mills, and mines, and over which many homes are dotted. As you go through the train to the dining car, where, in the glow of numerous electric lights, dinner is being served, the train dashes into a tunnel, and the mountain range is pierced.

Blazing fires showing through a succession of furnace doors, so close to the track that you can almost feel the breath of the flames as you speed past, tell you that you are now in the heart of the coke-burning country and the region where bituminous coal is mined in abundance. You are still at the table when Cresson, the most popular summer resort in Western Pennsylvania, flashes by.

If on your journey west, or your return journey east, you care to get an idea of a typical American mountain resort, you will find in Cresson a most excellent example. Situated as it is on the very crest of one of the Alleghenies, in the heart of this glorious mountain scenery, with the Horse-shoe Curve only a few miles away, the location, in point of beauty and healthfulness, is unsurpassed. The grounds of the hotel—an imposing structure, which, with its cottages, has accommodations for a thousand guests—cover an area of over five hundred acres, the greater part of which is a beautifully-graded lawn garnished with flower-beds and shrubbery and plentifully dotted with trees. The house itself is both capacious and comfortable, its sleeping-rooms are large and airy, its dining halls and parlors attractive in decoration and furnishing, and its *cuisine* equal to that of any summer hotel in America. Here, too, are to be found mineral springs of unquestioned efficacy, and every facility for enjoyment, from a livery stable to tennis courts.

Half an hour later, as you sip your after-dinner coffee, the conductor tells you that you are in the neighborhood of Johnstown, the ill-fated borough that was swept almost entirely out of existence a few years ago by the giving way of a poorly-constructed dam, which allowed the Conemaugh River to surge over the town in a devastating flood, causing the loss of several thousand lives and the destruction of millions of dollars worth of property.

As you pass into the smoking-room once more for another cigar, the apartment, under the radiance of the electric lights, seems to have taken on a cheerier aspect even than during the day. Your fellow-passengers, under the influence of a most

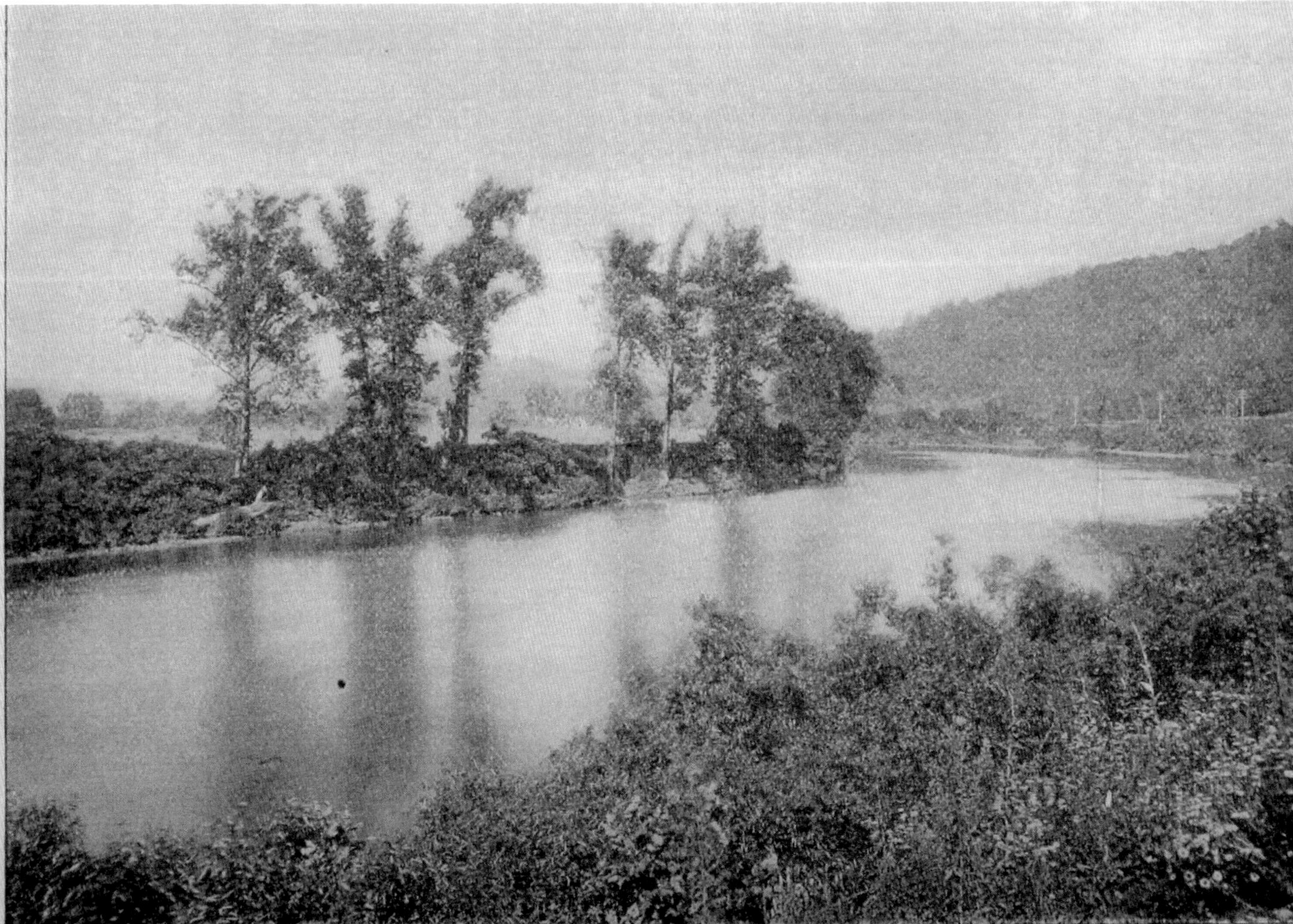

ON THE CONEMAUGH RIVER.

excellent dinner, have grown less reserved. A game of whist is in progress in one of the compartments between the smoking-room proper and the buffet beyond. Three or four men are discussing together the market prospects, taking their text from the closing prices of the day which were posted on the bulletin-board at Altoona; others are reading, and others still, with their heads close to the windows, are drinking in the beauty of the mountain scenery, which is now silvered by the pale light of the moon; and in this manner you yourself get an idea of the Pack-saddle narrows of the Conemaugh, the winding river below, and the wooded heights above.

An hour later your attention is attracted by towering columns of flame forming weird and fantastic arabesques against the night, and a communicative passenger tells you that the train has now reached the natural gas country. Village after village, illuminated by this means, is passed through, and then in the distance you descry the glimmering lights of Pittsburg. Your watch informs you that it is half-past nine when the train, on time to the minute, runs into the Union Depot in that city, which is the western terminus of the Pennsylvania Railroad proper, and you are puzzled for a moment to see by your time-table that you will leave for Chicago at 8.45. It is here that the Standard time changes. Heretofore you have reckoned your day by Eastern time; beyond Pittsburg you will reckon it by what is called Central time, which is an hour slower.

Here the dining car, which has served its purpose for the day, is taken off, and during the process you seize the opportunity to alight and indulge in a brisk walk up and down the station platform. From the depot you can get but a poor idea of the city. On your left rises a high hill, upon the top of which an electric light appears like a star in the black vault of the heavens, while on your right you see nothing but a succession of railroad tracks.

In point of fact, however, Pittsburg is a manufacturing city of no mean importance, and not only that, but a handsome city as well. Its natural beauties have been enhanced by public and private improvements. No more healthy city can be found in America, and in some of the essentials of comfort it has no rival. Natural gas is abundant, and is supplied at low rates for heating and cooking in private houses, as well as for manufacturing. Charitable, educational, and reformatory institutions abound, and its public edifices are numerous and imposing.

Soon after leaving Pittsburg you return to your sleeping car to find that the compartment allotted to you has been transformed into a most comfortable berth, hung with tapestry curtains. The linen is white and delicate, the pillows soft, and the coverings ample. The lights have been lowered, and when at last you decide to retire for the night, you confess that you are as well provided for as you could be under the roof of either hotel or private residence. Sleep quickly responds to your wooing ; and while you slumber your train glides smoothly over the tracks of the Pennsylvania's Western lines, across the State of Ohio, stopping at Alliance, Crestline, and Lima; and then into Indiana, where, just as the rising sun begins to tint the East with the first flush of a new day, another halt is made at Fort Wayne.

When you first open your eyes the flat country of the Hoosier State spreads itself out for miles before you, and you turn over for another nap, from which you are awakened by the voice of one of the dining car waiters, who is making known the fact to the sleeping passengers that breakfast is served. The car has been taken on at Fort Wayne, and when, having bathed in the bath-room, been shaved deftly by the barber, and finished your toilet in a lavatory, elaborately fitted up with basins of silver, you seek the breakfast-room, it is to discover a duplicate of the car that was left behind at Pittsburg the evening before.

Before you have finished your morning meal a line of dazzling, greenish blue suddenly shows itself off to the right. It is Lake Michigan, and already you are in the suburbs of Chicago. Railroad tracks innumerable spread themselves on either side of you; small stations at which local trains are standing, or from which they are just departing, flash by; buildings, ranging in size from modest cottages to mammoth warehouses, come and go; and a man in uniform comes through the car asking you to which hotel you wish to go, and how many trunks you have to be sent. He is the agent of an omnibus line and a local express company, and for a nominal sum will send both yourself and your luggage to your chosen destination. You hurry away to gather up your traps in the sleeping car, and just as you have your portmanteau strapped and your rugs rolled, the train glides into the depot at Chicago, and comes to a standstill—its journey over.

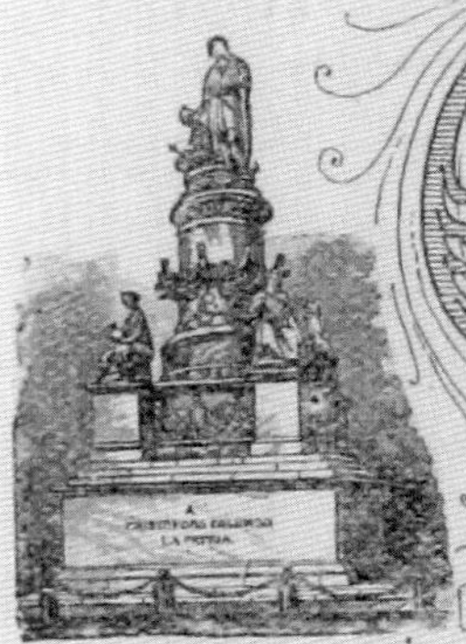

CHICAGO has been reached in the foregoing pages by means of the Pennsylvania Limited, and while this is the greatest it is by no means the only train which the matchless facilities of the Pennsylvania Railroad offer to the traveler. Another train, almost as perfect in appointment as the Limited, is the Columbian Express. This train, named in honor of the Great Fair, was added to the service as a relief to the Limited, on account of the increased traffic incident to the Exposition. It is composed of Pullman vestibule sleeping cars, dining cars, smoking cars, and passenger coaches, all constructed especially for this train. These cars are painted in the standard cardinal color of the Pennsylvania Railroad, and with their black and gold trimmings present a most attractive appearance to the eye. Inside they are finished in quiet colors, and furnished with all the comforts of cars of the highest class. The dining cars are available for all meals, so that every passenger, even though one should not choose to secure accommodations in the sleeping car, may take every meal *en route* without leaving the train.

The Columbian Express leaves New York in the early afternoon, traverses the State of New Jersey and all of Eastern Pennsylvania before the curtain of night descends to shut out the scenery. The traveler will miss the panoramic landscapes that Central and Western Pennsylvania unfolds to the patrons of the Limited, and, retiring in the mountains, will awake, if an early riser, in the neighborhood of the thriving town of Mansfield, in the State of Ohio. While eating your breakfast the unmistakable odor of petroleum will be wafted into the car for the nonce, and by this sign you will know the train is crossing the great oil-fields of Ohio, of which Lima is the centre. A couple of hours later Fort Wayne, Ind., one of the most important cities and the principal railroad centre between Pittsburg and Chicago, will be reached, and after a stop for exchanging locomotives the trip will be resumed. A glance at Plymouth, Ind., will be given as the train rushes through, and in two hours more the shores of Lake Michigan will be visible, and the interminable maze of railroad tracks that cover the surface of suburban Chicago will cause you to marvel how an engineman can guide his flying steed in safety through such a puzzling confusion of switches. A little more than twenty-five hours have elapsed since you left New York, when you disembark amid the bustle of the great Chicago Station.

It may happen that you will select a still later train from New York, one leaving towards six o'clock, and in that case the Western Express will be your choice. This train is exceedingly popular with business men, for the reason that it leaves the eastern metropolis after all the work of the day is ended. It is as comfortable in its equipment as the one just described, since it is composed of Pullman vestibule sleeping cars and dining cars. Its westward flight begins in the night, and the first light of day breaks through the window of your berth in Western Pennsylvania, near Pittsburg. You get a passing glimpse of the great Iron City and its twin sister, Allegheny, the two separated by the Allegheny River; you bisect the great State of Ohio, with its diversified industries clearly manifested in the country and towns which mark the line, and in the waning afternoon you cross the boundary line and enter Indiana. After twilight you glide across the corner of Illinois, and stop in Chicago as the chimes on the station tower is telling the hour—9.30 of the evening.

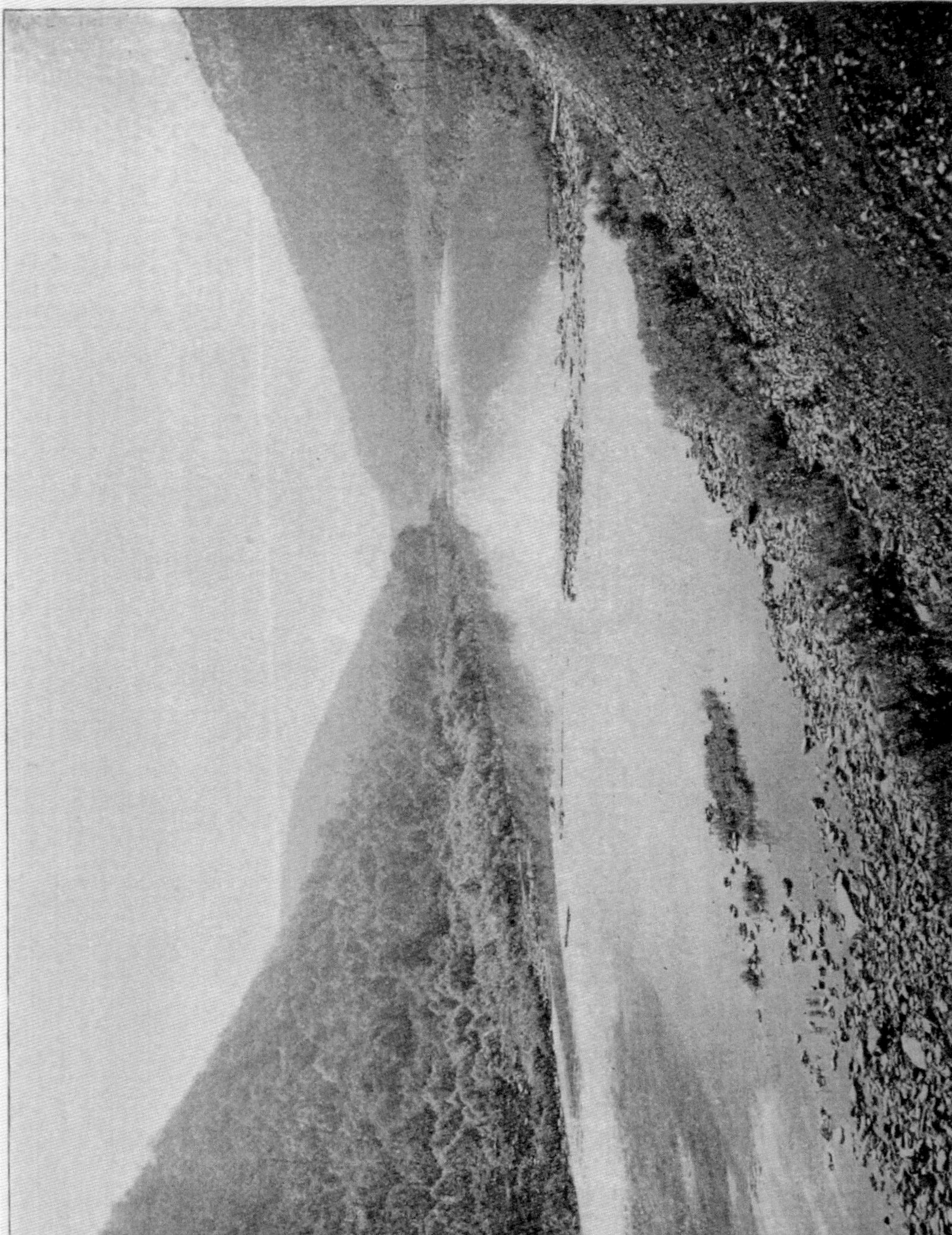

The real night train for Chicago, however, leaves New York at eight o'clock in the evening. There is no lack of comfortable accommodation on this, which is known as the Pacific Express. This is in some respects the most notable train of the service. It is distinctively the scenic train of the line, as it reaches the mountains in the morning and crosses the Alleghenies when the skies are lighted with the radiance of the rising sun and the air is redolent with the freshness of a new day. The act of awakening amid such scenes is at first startling in its effects, but the breath of the mountains and the grandeur of the scenery in the full flush of early sunlight is full recompense for the loss of an hour or so of slumber. By this train breakfast is taken at Altoona, the mountain workshop of the Pennsylvania Railroad, and after an excellent meal at the Logan House the train proceeds. An observation car is here attached, and an additional locomotive to aid in overcoming the steep grade.

Within a few minutes the Horse-shoe Curve is sighted, and a thrill of admiration, which expands into a feeling of wonder and delight, takes possession of every one who looks upon the scenes of wild beauty which are presented on every hand. It is a magnificent spectacle, and one which will cling to the memory forever.

The entire western portion of the State of Pennsylvania, with its fiery coke-ovens, smoking furnaces, and flaming gas-wells, will be traversed by daylight, as well as the eastern portion of the State of Ohio as far as Mansfield. Then the shadows of night lengthen into darkness, and the traveler will retire on the train to awaken in the early morning at his destination—the city of the World's Fair.

Assuming that you have traveled direct from New York to Chicago by any one of the trains described, it would be an excellent idea to vary the return trip by a visit to the National Capital. This may be accomplished in the most satisfactory manner by taking at Chicago any one of the celebrated trains of the Pennsylvania System. These trains leave Chicago at different hours during the day, and carry cars through to Washington as well as to New York. The route is the same as west-bound from Chicago to Harrisburg, Pa. There the lines diverge, and the Washington portion of the train is separated from the New York section and is forwarded to the National Capital over another branch of the Pennsylvania System. The line to Washington shortly after leaving Harrisburg is carried over the Susquehanna by a substantial viaduct, and follows the banks of the picturesque stream for many miles. It also traverses one of the most attractive and productive agricultural sections of the Union, wherein green hills and flowery meadows serve to diversify the landscape. York, one of the oldest and thriftiest towns in the State, devoted largely to manufacturing enterprises, is the principal city passed, and shortly after it vanishes in the distance the boundary of the State of Maryland is crossed. A beautiful stretch of country spreads out from both sides of the railway, until the train enters the prosperous commercial city of Baltimore. One may well break the journey here, if one cares to see the most interesting city of the upper South. Its handsome harbor, protected by the guns of the historic Fort McHenry, its grain elevators, its monuments, its busy streets and beautiful parks, will well repay the time devoted to their inspection.

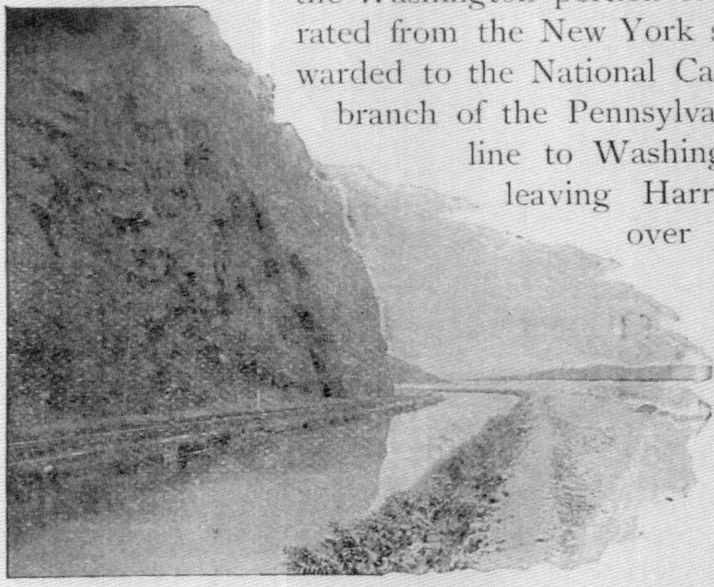

Leaving the Union Station at Baltimore the train proceeds under the city, through a succession of tunnels, out into a flat and uninteresting country for an hour's ride until the white dome of the Capitol is outlined against the horizon, and you recognize the fact that the capital of the United States has been reached.

Returning to New York from Washington still another portion of the Pennsylvania System offers its superior facilities. Trains leave for Philadelphia and New York at almost every hour of the day, and among them are some of the best examples of the most completely-equipped fast trains of this great railway.

In describing the route to Chicago it has been assumed that the traveler would go direct from New York to the World's Fair City and visit the other cities as he leisurely returns to the East. This is by no means necessary, and the reverse order may as well be followed. The Chicago ticket will admit of a break in the journey at any one or all of the points mentioned, and the traveler may use his own discretion in stopping either as he goes west or on the eastward trip.

In the following pages descriptive notes of the principal cities *en route* between New York and Chicago are given.

The descriptive notes, brief as they are, will doubtless serve to whet the curiosity, and at the same time help the traveler to see all the points of interest in each city to the best advantage.

PHILADELPHIA.

CENTRALLY located in the very heart of the great Quaker City in the midst of its most notable architectural section, there is no handsomer nor better-appointed railroad station in America than the Broad Street Station of the Pennsylvania Railroad Company at Philadelphia, into which you are whirled over an elevated road-bed that extends from beyond the Schuylkill River, the western boundary of the city proper, a mile and a half away. Constructed of granite, ornamental brick, and terra cotta in a picturesque combination of the gothic, Greek, and Roman styles of architecture, its general beauty is enhanced by a lofty clock tower which rises from its northeastern corner. As you come down its broad sweep of stone steps and out upon South Broad Street, a mammoth pile of white marble rises up across the way, dwarfing the station with which it is in most pronounced contrast, and like a mighty fortress seeming to challenge your entrance to the city of the Quakers. It is the new City Hall, and admittedly the largest public building in the United States, not even excepting the Capitol building at Washington. Situated at the intersection of two of Philadelphia's widest and most important thoroughfares, Broad Street and Market Street, it may be said to mark the centre of the city proper, both geographically and in point of population. It has been in course of construction since 1871, and it is still by no means near completion. It covers an area of four and one-half acres, not including the court-yard, two hundred feet square, which is in its centre, nor the grand avenue, two hundred and five feet wide on the northern front and one hundred and thirty-five feet wide on the others, which surrounds it. It contains

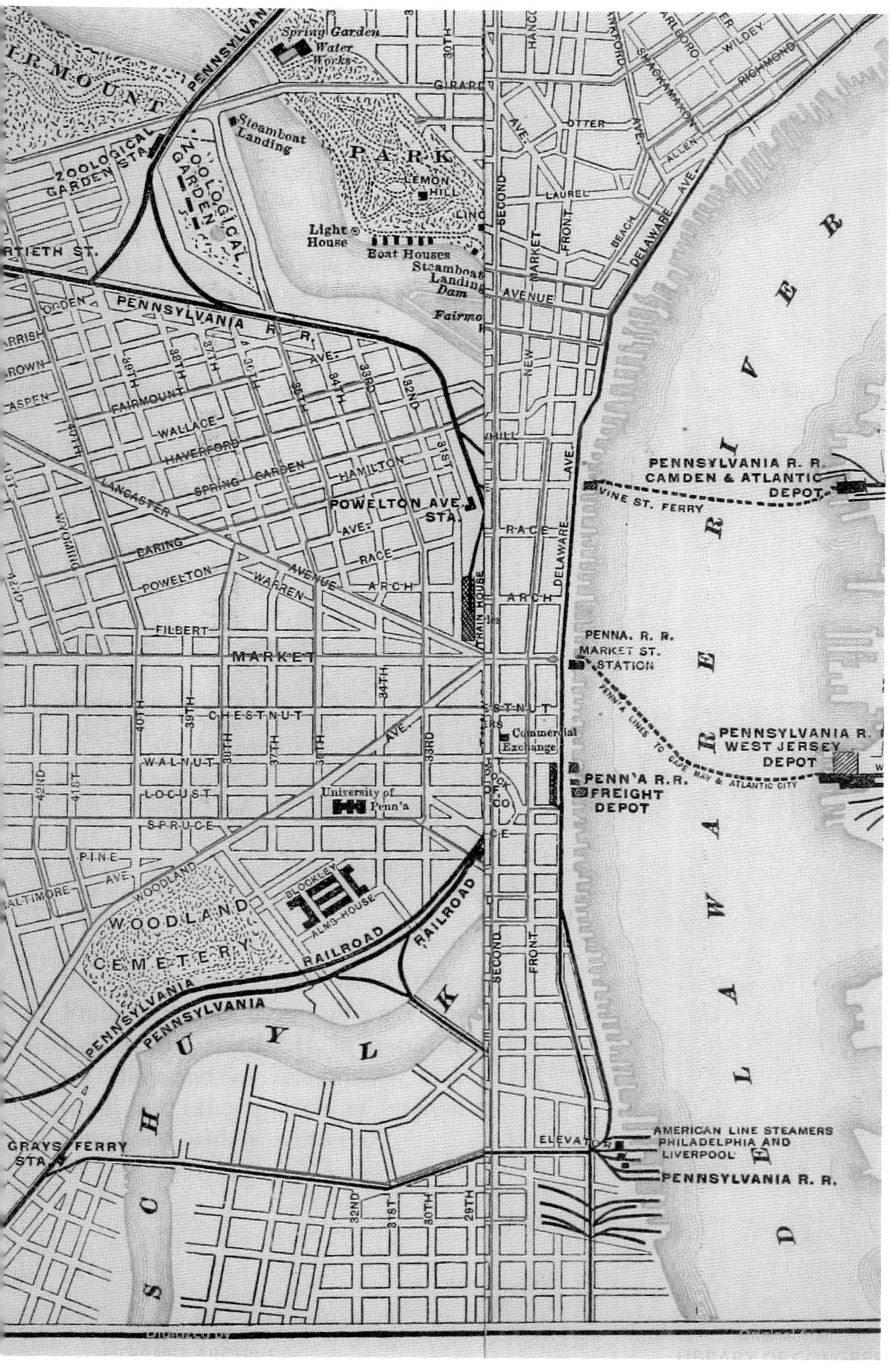
FAIRMOUNT
PARK
PENNSYLVANIA
Spring Garden Water Works
GIRARD
Steamboat Landing
ZOOLOGICAL GARDEN STA.
ZOOLOGICAL GARDEN
LEMON HILL
Light House
Boat Houses
Steamboat Landing
Dam
FORTIETH ST.
OGDEN
PENNSYLVANIA R. R.
PARRISH
BROWN
ASPEN
FAIRMOUNT
WALLACE
HAVERFORD
SPRING GARDEN
HAMILTON
LANCASTER
POWELTON AVE. STA.
BARING
POWELTON
WARREN
AVENUE
RACE
ARCH
FILBERT
MARKET
CHESTNUT
WALNUT
LOCUST
SPRUCE
PINE
BALTIMORE
WOODLAND
University of Penn'a
BLOCKLEY ALMS-HOUSE
WOODLAND CEMETERY
PENNSYLVANIA RAILROAD
RAILROAD
SCHUYLKILL
GRAYS FERRY STA.
TRAIN HOUSE
Commercial Exchange
SECOND
FRONT
NEW
MARKET
HANCOCK
FRANKFORD AVE.
MARLBORO
SHACKAMAXON
WILDEY
RICHMOND
OTTER
LAUREL
BEACH
ALLEN
DELAWARE AVE.
AVENUE
PENNSYLVANIA R. R. CAMDEN & ATLANTIC DEPOT
VINE ST. FERRY
PENNA. R. R. MARKET ST. STATION
PENN'A LINES TO CAPE MAY & ATLANTIC CITY
PENNSYLVANIA R. R. WEST JERSEY DEPOT
PENN'A R.R. FREIGHT DEPOT
ELEVATOR
AMERICAN LINE STEAMERS PHILADELPHIA AND LIVERPOOL
PENNSYLVANIA R. R.
DELAWARE RIVER
42ND
41ST
40TH
39TH
38TH
37TH
36TH
35TH
34TH
33RD
32ND
31ST
30TH
29TH

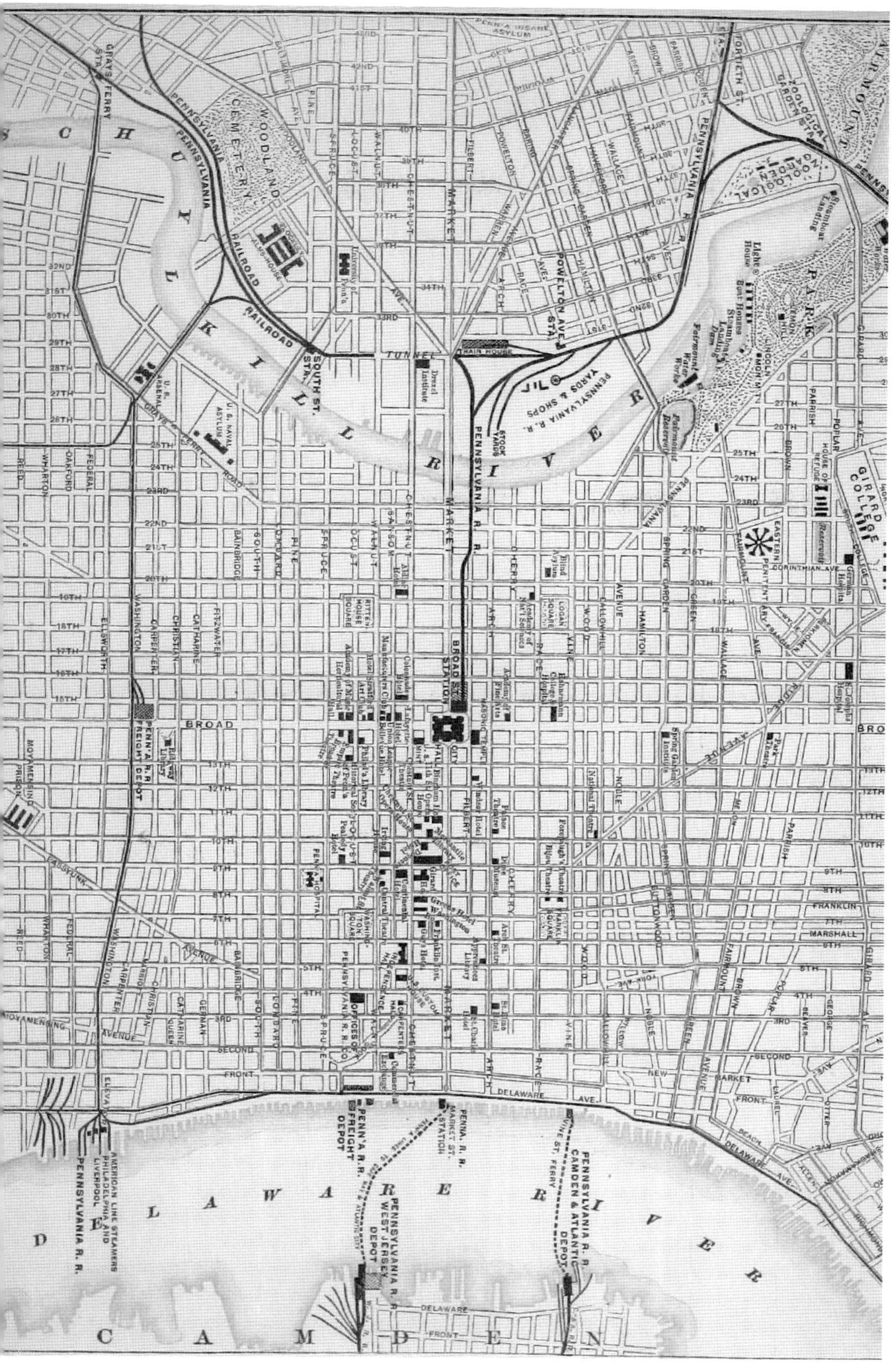

SCHUYLKILL RIVER
DELAWARE RIVER
CAMDEN
WOODLAND CEMETERY
PENNSYLVANIA RAILROAD
PENNSYLVANIA R.R.
FAIRMOUNT PARK
ZOOLOGICAL GARDEN
ZOOLOGICAL GARDEN STA.
GIRARD COLLEGE
EASTERN PENITENTIARY
BROAD ST. STATION
CITY HALL
TRAIN HOUSE
TUNNEL
SOUTH ST. STA.
POWELTON AVE. STA.
PENNSYLVANIA R.R. YARDS & SHOPS
STOCK YARDS
DREXEL INSTITUTE
U.S. ARSENAL
U.S. NAVAL ASYLUM
PENNSYLVANIA HOSPITAL
MOYAMENSING PRISON
PENN'A R.R. FREIGHT DEPOT
PENNSYLVANIA R.R. CAMDEN & ATLANTIC DEPOT
PENNSYLVANIA R.R. WEST JERSEY DEPOT
PENNA. R.R. MARKET ST. STATION
VINE ST. FERRY
AMERICAN LINE STEAMERS PHILADELPHIA AND LIVERPOOL
OFFICES OF PENNSYLVANIA R.R. CO.
MARKET
BROAD
DELAWARE AVE.
PENNA INSANE ASYLUM

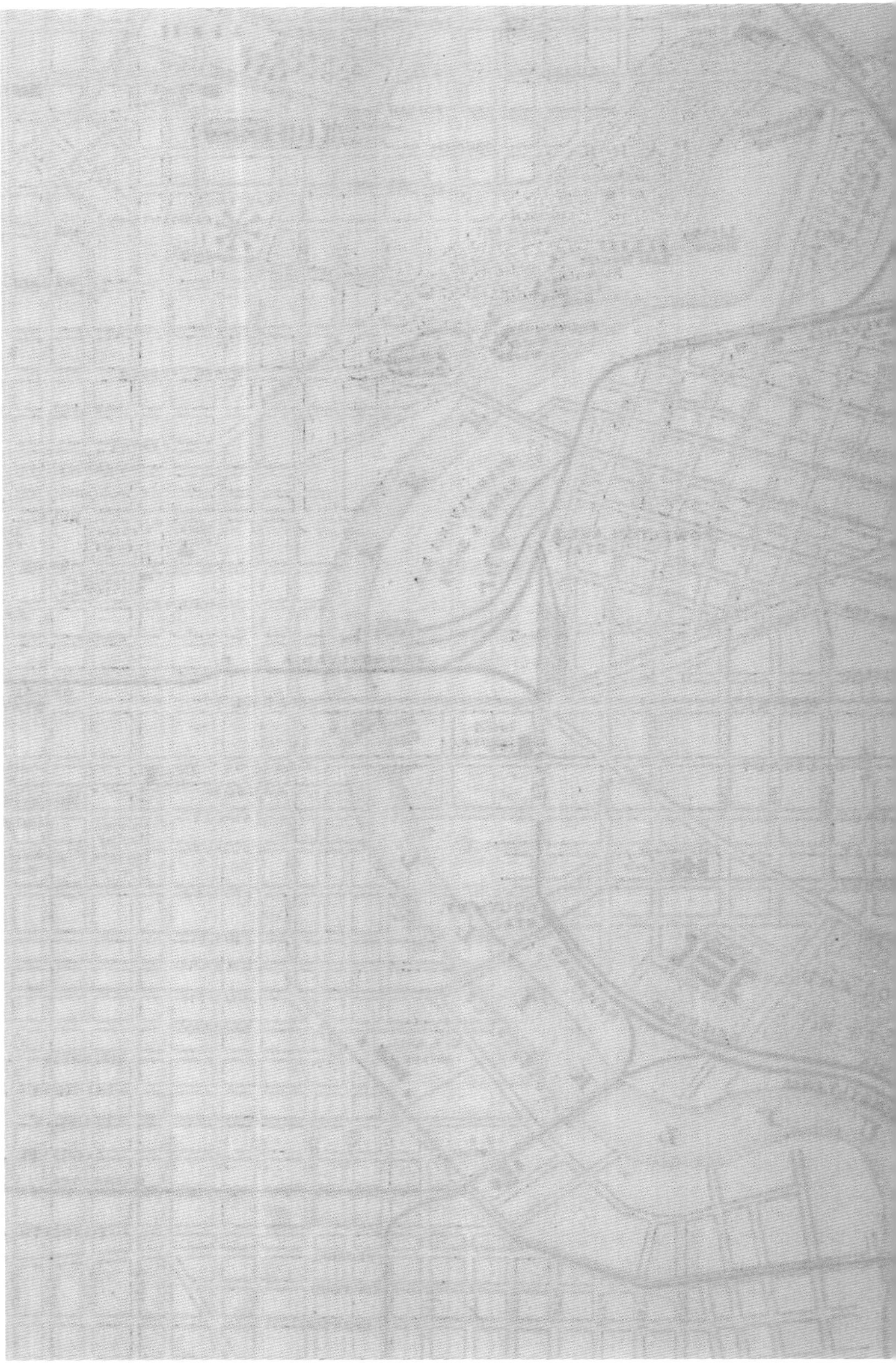

five hundred and twenty rooms, and accommodates not only the municipal offices, but the chambers of the Supreme Court of Pennsylvania. The tower, which rises from the middle of its northern side, will, when completed, reach a height of five hundred and thirty-seven feet, terminating in a colossal statue of William Penn, the founder of the city. Chestnut Street, on or near which the principal hotels are situated, is a block and a half to your right as you make your exit from the station, and a Pennsylvania Railroad hansom, a number of which are always in waiting in the court to your left as you descend to the street, will for fifty cents take you to any hotel within a mile that you may select, all of which are noted on the map of the city. The points of interest in Philadelphia from a purely historical standpoint are nearly all to be found between the new City Hall and the Delaware River, which bounds the city on the east, but Philadelphia is geographically the largest city in the Union, as well as the third city in population, with its one million forty-six thousand of inhabitants, and its landmarks, public institutions, and other objects of interest to the visitor are of necessity somewhat widely scattered.

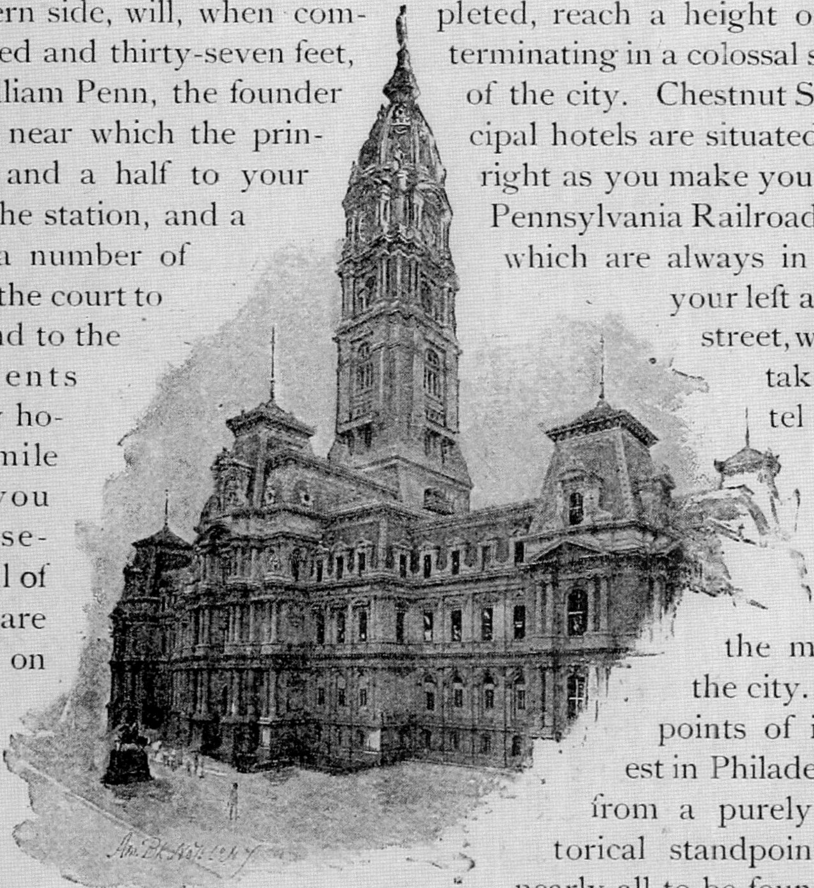

CITY HALL, PHILADELPHIA.

Historically, Philadelphia is the most important of American cities. Here it was that the first gathering of representatives from the American Colonies was held, in 1774; here it was that the Second Continental Congress declared the Colonies' independence, and here it was that the original seat of government of the United States was established. A walk of a few blocks down Chestnut Street from your hotel, past the principal shops, newspaper offices, and monetary institutions of the city, will bring you to the old State House, now called Independence Hall, wherein the Declaration of Independence was signed. The building occupies the middle of the block between Fifth and Sixth Streets, and it is flanked on either sides by smaller red brick structures, in the same general quaintly plain style of architecture, and which are used as offices, court-rooms, and halls of record by

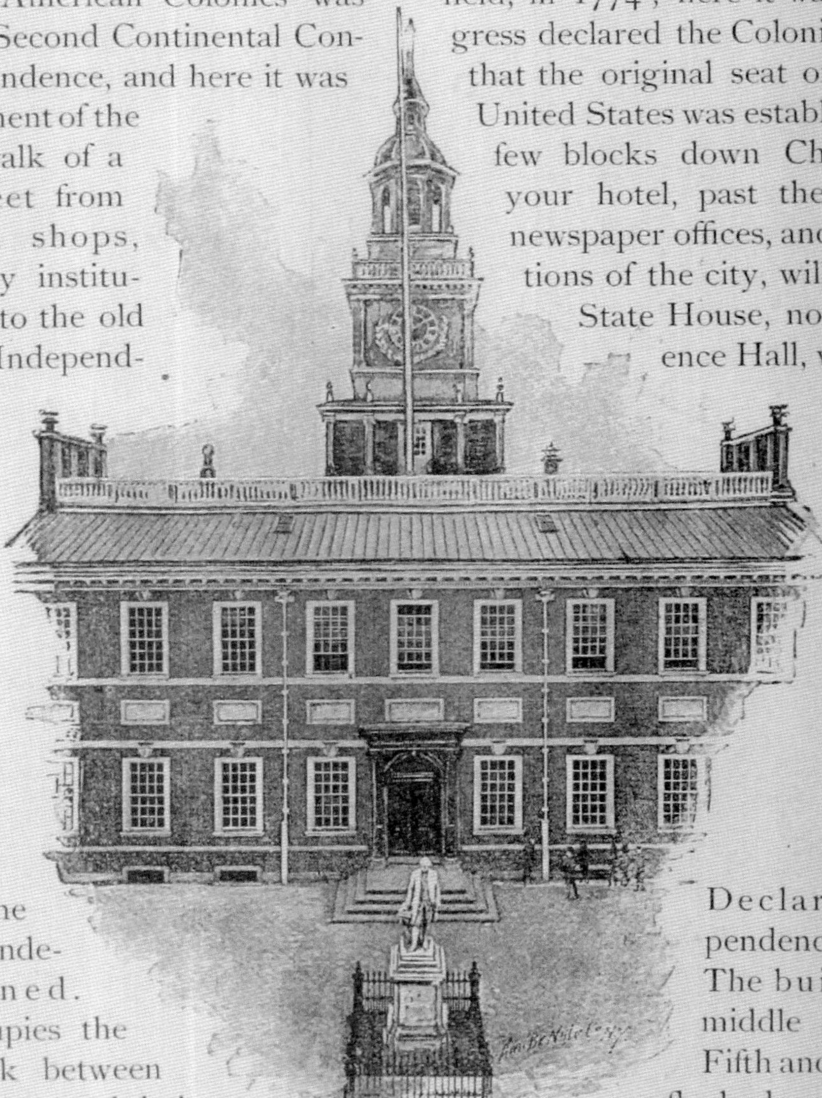

INDEPENDENCE HALL.

the city government. Within the southern vestibule of Independence Hall, and beneath the tower in which it originally hung, is the old bell which proclaimed liberty to the American people, and in a museum which occupies one of the rooms on the ground floor are to be seen many relics of Revolutionary days. In the room opposite are portraits of the signers of the Declaration, the table upon which the instrument was signed, and other furniture which had a place in the halls of Congress at that time. The upper rooms are used as the City Council chambers pending the removal of that body to the new City Hall. In the rear is Independence Square.

Carpenters' Hall stands back from Chestnut Street two blocks farther east, in the rear of an ornate banking building, and is reached through a narrow court-way. In architecture it is similar to the State House, but much smaller, and presents its gable end to the street. Here the first Continental Congress assembled, and here, as an inscription on the wall will tell you, "Henry, Hancock, and Adams inspired the delegates of the Colonies with nerve and sinew for the toils of war." It was built in 1770, and was first intended only for the uses of the Society of Carpenters, by whom it was founded. Its interior has been restored to as nearly as possible its original revolutionary aspect, and its walls are hung with relics of that period.

Christ Church, where in colonial days the royal officers attended divine worship, and where, after the Revolutionary war, the President and other officers of the United States had pews, is three blocks northeast from Carpenters' Hall, on Second Street above Market. Like the buildings already mentioned, it is of red brick, and was built in 1727–31 on the site of the original church erected in 1695. Its steeple contains a chime of bells cast in London about the middle of the last century.

Another old church well worth inspection lies about a mile to the south and just off Second Street. It is known as the Old

Swedes' Church, and was built in 1700 by the Scandinavian settlers to take the place of a log structure erected in 1677, four years before the landing of Penn, which served as both a place of worship and a fort. The old grave-yard which surrounds it is particularly interesting. St. Peter's Church, at Third and Pine Streets, and the Pine Street Presbyterian Church, at Fourth and Pine Streets, are ecclesiastical structures that likewise date back to colonial times.

On your way back to your hotel you may pass the Pennsylvania Hospital building, which occupies, with its grounds, the entire block bounded by Eighth and Ninth and Spruce and Pine Streets, and which is one of the finest examples of colonial architecture still in existence. Built in 1755, the first clinical lectures given in America were delivered within its walls.

Returning to Chestnut Street there are two or three objects of interest that have thus far escaped you. It is possible that in going from the State House to Carpenters' Hall you have noticed a marble structure just east of Fifth Street resembling the Parthenon at Athens, and have learned that, originally erected for the Second United States Bank in 1819–1824, it is now occupied by the Collector of Customs for the Port of Philadelphia and the Assistant Treasurer of the United States. You have, too, in all probability, observed the Drexel Building adjoining it and extending to the corner of Fifth Street, in which the Philadelphia Stock Exchange has its quarters; but you have not yet had pointed out to you the mammoth gray stone building at the corner of Ninth Street, popularly called the Post-Office, but which contains also the United States Court Rooms, and branch offices of the Coast Survey, Geological Survey, the Light-House Board, and of the Secret and Signal Service of the Government. Including the site, the building cost nearly $8,000,000. The United States Mint is about four blocks farther west, and is a most interesting place to visit.

Having strolled from one end of Chestnut Street to the other, a ride south on Broad Street as far as the Ridgway Library would reward you with a view of one of Philadelphia's most imposing edifices, a branch of the Philadelphia Library (a free institution that dates back to the time of Franklin), and the outcome of a legacy of more than a million dollars left by Dr. John Rush, who, with his wife, after whom it is named, lies buried within its walls.

North Broad Street would also well repay a visit. Beyond the new City Hall is the Masonic Temple, a granite structure of large dimensions and ornamental design. The somewhat ornate home of the Pennsylvania Academy of Fine Arts, with one of the finest picture galleries in the country and a most admirable art school, occupies a corner one block farther north. In the next block is the Hahnemann Medical College and Hospital, and then Broad Street is, for a time, given up to manufactories, including, among others, the Baldwin Locomotive Works. A few squares north of this begins the residence part of the street, where many of the most beautiful dwellings in the city are located.

About a mile to the west, leaving Broad Street at Girard Avenue, you will find Girard College, with its forty acres of land, and its several more or less picturesque buildings. This is an educational institution for orphan boys, founded and endowed by the late Stephen Girard.

Philadelphia's chief educational institution—the University of Pennsylvania—is situated west of the Schuylkill River, in what is known as West Philadelphia. Its buildings are large and its grounds ample. It was first chartered in 1753, and the growth in value since that time of the land that forms its endowment has rendered possible its elevation to its present proud position. Of its schools, which include almost every department of education, the most celebrated is that of medicine, which ranks with the best in the world.

On your way to the University, at Chestnut and Thirty-third Streets you will observe the handsome new building of the Drexel Institute. It was constructed and endowed by the munificence of the eminent banker, Mr. A. J. Drexel, and its object is the training of the young of both sexes in the paths of industry and art. It is a magnificent charity. The museum contains many rare objects, and its library many books and manuscripts that cannot be found elsewhere.

Philadelphia's clubs, like its other institutions, are pretty well scattered over its broad surface, but its principal ones are within a short distance of Broad and Walnut Streets. Here are the Philadelphia Club, the oldest and most exclusive; the Union League, the wealthiest; the Art, the University, the Rittenhouse, and the Manufacturers'.

In Fairmount Park Philadelphia possesses one of the largest and most beautiful public pleasure-grounds in the world. Extending for seven miles along both sides of the Schuylkill River and six miles along Wissahickon Creek, it is rich in natural scenery of a most picturesque description. Its Zoological Gardens are the finest in America, and it contains in its relics of the Centennial Exposition of 1876 some highly attractive features. Among the private residences of colonial days that are within its borders are Mount Pleasant, once the home of Benedict Arnold, and Belmont Mansion, where Judge Peters entertained Washington and Lafayette. The brick house that William Penn built for himself near Second and Market Streets has been removed to the Park, and is an interesting landmark on one of its principal drives.

Days might be spent with profit among the numerous manufacturing establishments of Philadelphia, for it is a manufacturing city primarily; and it possesses also numerous educational, charitable, religious, and other institutions that will yield a good return for the time devoted to their inspection.

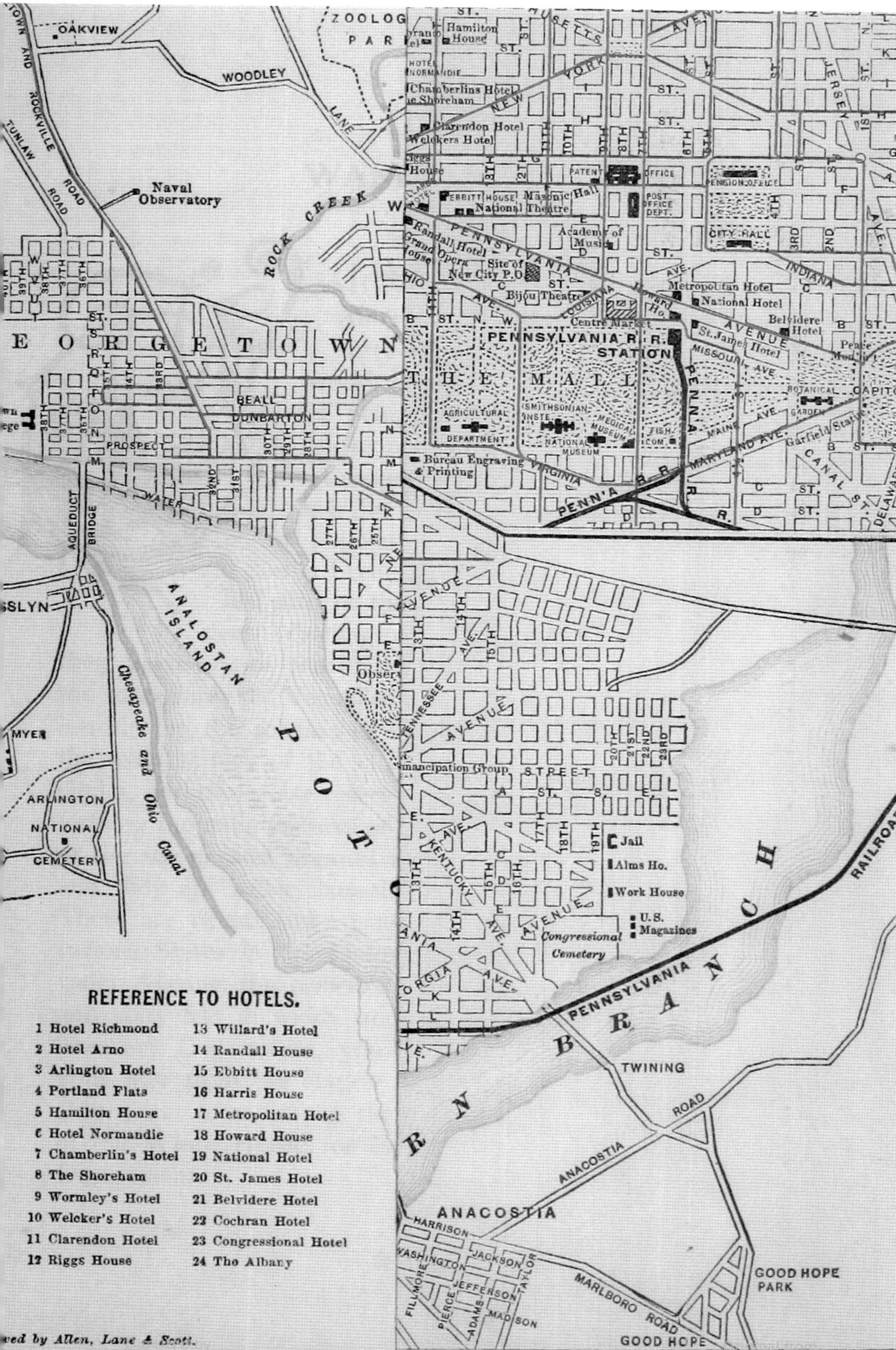
REFERENCE TO HOTELS.
1 Hotel Richmond
2 Hotel Arno
3 Arlington Hotel
4 Portland Flats
5 Hamilton House
6 Hotel Normandie
7 Chamberlin's Hotel
8 The Shoreham
9 Wormley's Hotel
10 Welcker's Hotel
11 Clarendon Hotel
12 Riggs House
13 Willard's Hotel
14 Randall House
15 Ebbitt House
16 Harris House
17 Metropolitan Hotel
18 Howard House
19 National Hotel
20 St. James Hotel
21 Belvidere Hotel
22 Cochran Hotel
23 Congressional Hotel
24 The Albany
OAKVIEW
WOODLEY
LANE
TUNLAW
ROCKVILLE ROAD
Naval Observatory
ROCK CREEK
GEORGETOWN
BEALL
DUNBARTON
PROSPECT
WATER
AQUEDUCT BRIDGE
ANALOSTAN ISLAND
Chesapeake and Ohio Canal
MYER
ARLINGTON NATIONAL CEMETERY
Hamilton House
Hotel Normandie
Chamberlins Hotel
The Shoreham
Clarendon Hotel
Welckers Hotel
Riggs House
Ebbitt House
Masonic Hall
National Theatre
Patent Office
Post Office Dept.
Pension Office
City Hall
Academy of Music
Randall Hotel
Grand Opera House
Site of New City P.O.
Bijou Theatre
Metropolitan Hotel
National Hotel
Howard Ho.
Centre Market
Belvidere Hotel
St. James Hotel
PENNSYLVANIA R. R. STATION
THE MALL
Agricultural Department
Smithsonian Inste.
National Museum
Medical Museum
Fish Com.
Botanical Garden
Capitol
Garfield Statue
Peace Mon't
Bureau Engraving & Printing
PENNSYLVANIA AVENUE
INDIANA
MISSOURI AVE.
MAINE AVE.
MARYLAND AVE.
VIRGINIA
PENN'A R. R.
CANAL ST.
DELAWARE
NEW YORK
NEW JERSEY
TENNESSEE AVENUE
KENTUCKY AVE.
Emancipation Group
Jail
Alms Ho.
Work House
U.S. Magazines
Congressional Cemetery
PENNSYLVANIA
RAILROAD
EASTERN BRANCH
TWINING
ANACOSTIA ROAD
ANACOSTIA
HARRISON
WASHINGTON
JACKSON
JEFFERSON
TAYLOR
FILLMORE
PIERCE
ADAMS
MADISON
MARLBORO ROAD
GOOD HOPE
GOOD HOPE PARK
...ved by Allen, Lane & Scott.

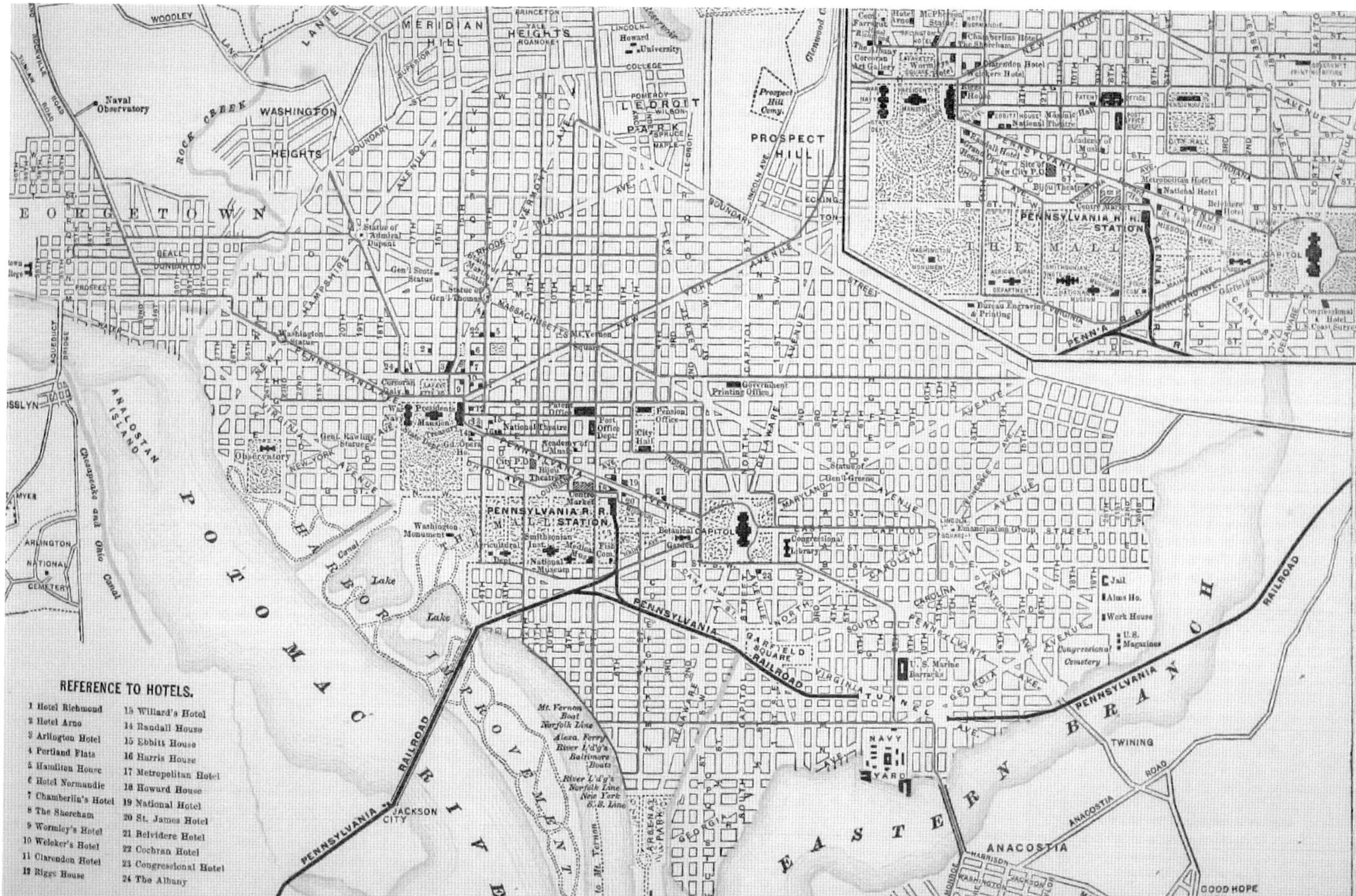
REFERENCE TO HOTELS.
1 Hotel Richmond
2 Hotel Arno
3 Arlington Hotel
4 Portland Flats
5 Hamilton House
6 Hotel Normandie
7 Chamberlin's Hotel
8 The Shoreham
9 Wormley's Hotel
10 Welcker's Hotel
11 Clarendon Hotel
12 Riggs House
13 Willard's Hotel
14 Randall House
15 Ebbitt House
16 Harris House
17 Metropolitan Hotel
18 Howard House
19 National Hotel
20 St. James Hotel
21 Belvidere Hotel
22 Cochran Hotel
23 Congressional Hotel
24 The Albany
GEORGETOWN
WASHINGTON HEIGHTS
MERIDIAN HILL
LEDROIT PARK
PROSPECT HILL
POTOMAC RIVER
EASTERN BRANCH
ANACOSTIA
ANALOSTAN ISLAND
PENNSYLVANIA RAILROAD
CAPITOL
NAVY YARD
THE MALL
Naval Observatory
Howard University
Washington Monument
Chesapeake and Ohio Canal
ARLINGTON NATIONAL CEMETERY
JACKSON CITY

WASHINGTON.

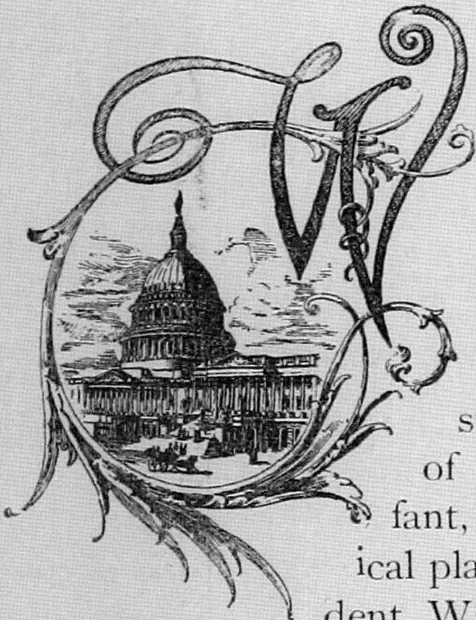

WASHINGTON, peculiarly unlike ar American city, is also in striking larity to the other National capitals world. It was created for the sole of being the seat of Government, consequently in marked contrast wit European capitals which were ch such because of their pre-eminence i of population and commerce. Majo fant, a French engineer, prepared the top ical plan of the city under the direction c dent Washington and Thomas Jefferson, w then Secretary of State, and took as his basis for the the topography of Versailles, the seat of government of introducing the scheme of broad transverse avenues inte the main streets of the city, with constantly recurring circles, and triangular reservations, which you will find at forming the main features of the city plan. The aggregat of the streets and avenues is two hundred and sixty-fou and they are wider than those of any other city in th There are twenty-one avenues in all, which bear the r various States in the Union, and along one of these, vania Avenue, the principal street of Washington, one and sixty feet in width, and extending from the Capitc Treasury Department, you are almost certain to be d your way from the station to your hotel, which you w ably select from among the group located in the neigh of the White House, or Executive Mansion, and the

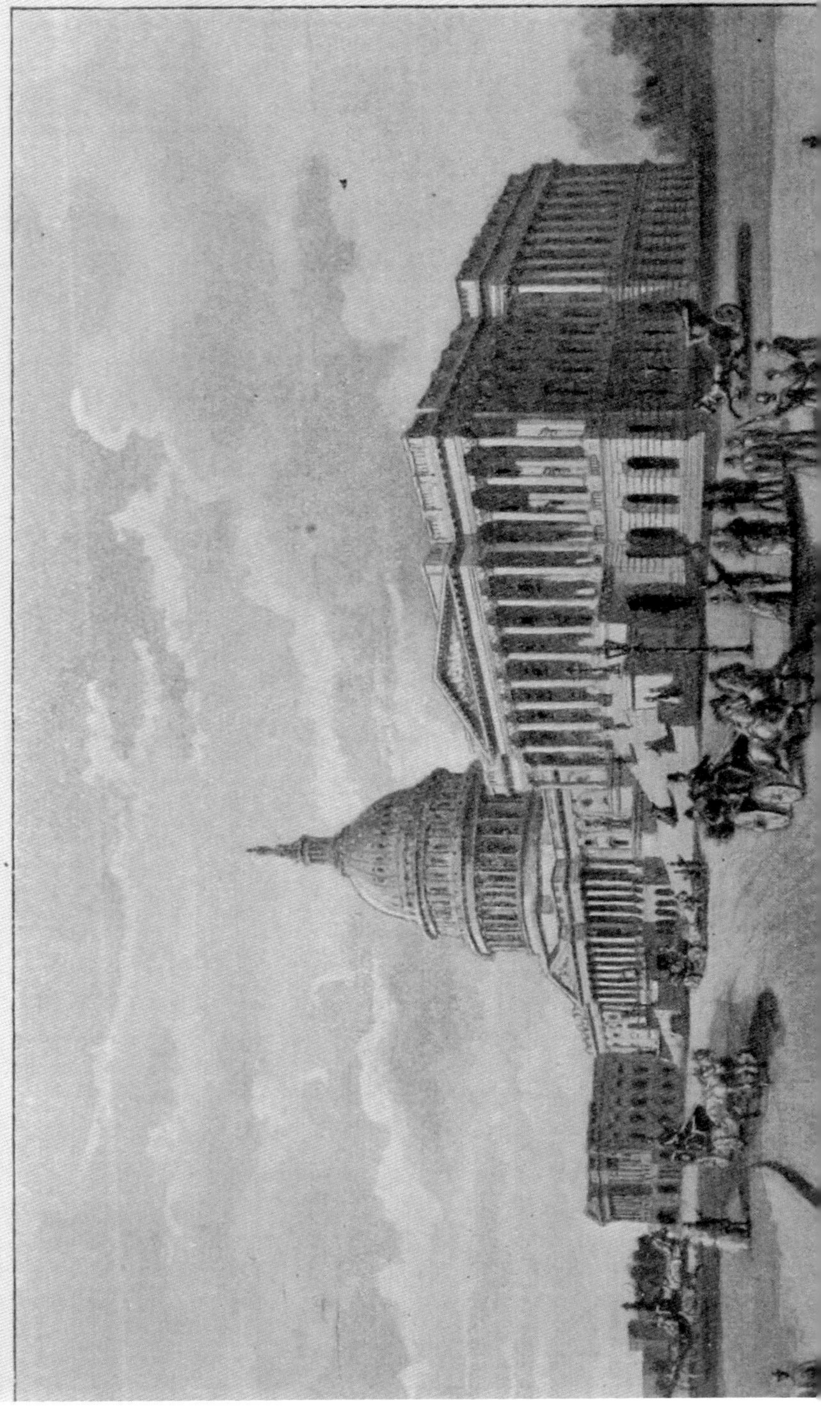

The principal show-place in Washington is the Cap dome of which you have already seen from a distance long-range view of which you have perhaps caught as yo into Pennsylvania Avenue. A street car of the Washing Georgetown line, or a Herdic coach, on either of which is five cents, lands you at the western front of this buildi as you mount the grand stairway and architectural terr walk around the Capitol to the east, you for the first time ate the colossal proportions of this council hall of the lawmakers, and are quite prepared to be told that it hundred and fifty-one feet long by three hundred and four feet broad; that it covers an area of three and a ha and that its dome rises three hundred and ninety-seven fe low tide in the Potomac; nor are you, as you gaze u graceful proportions of its white marble walls and pillars, s to learn that it has secured the almost unanimous prais best judges of all countries as the most impressive moder in the world. You examine with some care the statuar adorns the portico, and the great bronze doors by R Rogers, representing, in *alto-relievo*, events in the life of bus and the discovery of America, and then you pass rotunda, which forms the central attraction of the Capit which consists of a circular hall, ninety-six feet in diam one hundred and eighty feet in height to the canopy a which is painted a mammoth fresco by Brumidi, repr allegorical and historical subjects. Paintings of scenes f history of the nation also adorn the eight panels of the su ing wall.

Passing from the rotunda by the west door you re Library of Congress, which, with its six hundred and fif sand volumes and three hundred thousand pamphlets, largest library in the United States, and the fifth largest the Supreme Court, with its marble busts of the Chief Justices of the United States, and from here also rises the stairway that leads to the dome, from which, if you care to climb to it, a panorama of unexampled beauty may be witnessed. Statuary Hall, on the other side of the rotunda, contains a collection of statues of the prominent soldiers, jurists, and statesmen of each State.

In the north wing of the Capitol is the Senate Chamber, the niches in the galleries of which are embellished with marble busts of the Vice-Presidents. In this wing also are the President's room, the Vice-President's room,'the Marble Room, or Senators' reception-room, and the several Senate committee-rooms. In the south wing is the Hall of Representatives, surrounded by the Speaker's room, the House library, and the House committee-rooms. The grand stairways, leading from the several stories of the building, all bear striking decorations, while the walls and ceilings of the corridors, as well as of nearly every room, are celebrated for the frescoes with which they are illuminated.

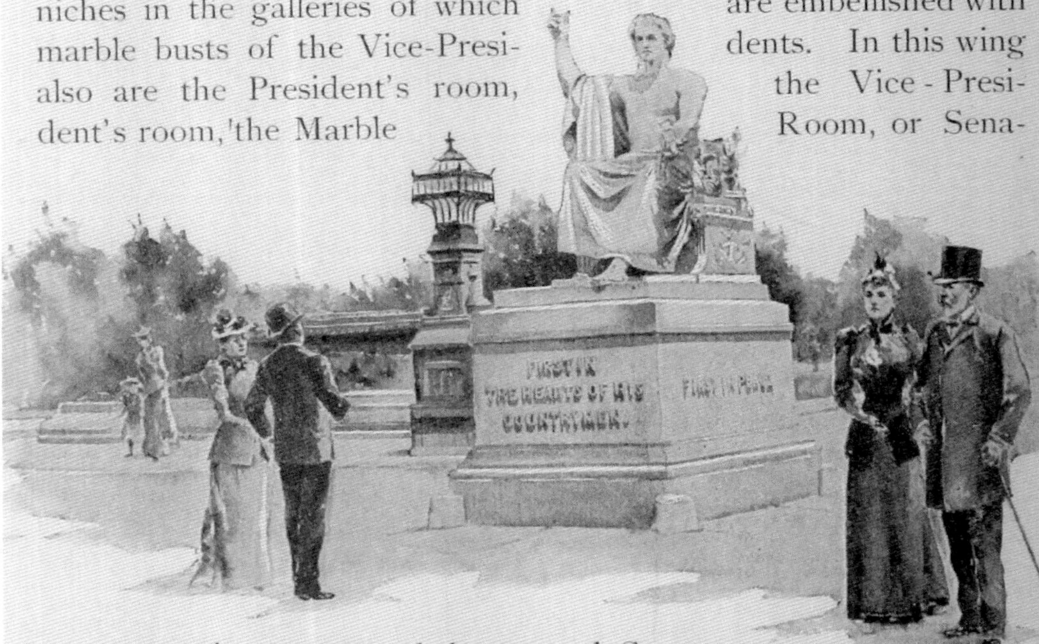

In leaving the Capitol you pass out of the western door and, descending the grand stairway, with its wealth of sculptured adornment, take the broad walk to the right leading to the Botanic Gardens, where you find in the conservatories some rare examples of the *flora* of the tropics.

The Executive Mansion, the home of the President of the United States, commonly spoken of as the White House, lies at the other end of Pennsylvania Avenue, between the Treasury building and that of the War, State, and Navy Departments. It is a plain, stately structure of freestone, painted white, with a colonnade of eight simple Ionic columns in front and a semi-circular portico in the rear, and surrounded by grounds which are given the semblance of a park by means of an array of fountains, flowers, and shrubbery. The East Room is the one room in the house that is open to visitors—a large, lofty apartment, decorated in the Greek style. Upon its walls are the portraits of Washington, Jefferson, Lincoln, and Mrs. Washington. The other rooms on the ground floor—the Blue Room, Green Room, and State dining-rooms, you find closed to you unless you have special permission to visit them. On the upper floor are the President's office and those of his Secretaries, together with the apartments of the Presidential family.

From the rear windows of the White House a view is had of the Washington obelisk, or national monument. It is the loftiest construction of masonry in the world, the shaft of Maryland marble rising to a height of five hundred and fifty-five feet.

The mighty pile of granite, iron, and slate which you notice on your left as you leave the White House consists of four harmonious buildings, united by connecting wings, and contains the offices of the War, Navy, and State Departments. It covers four and one-half acres; its corridors combined are over two miles in length, and its total cost was nearly $11,000,000.

The Department of State, which is in the south wing, you visit first, taking the elevator to the Library on the third floor, where you are shown the original draft of the Declaration of

Independence, the desk upon which it was written, and the original engrossed and signed copy, a case of historic relics, and other objects of interest. The fifty thousand volumes in the Library, including the works of the great writers of all ages on international affairs, statutes, and State papers, treaties, leagues, manifestos, and correspondence, make the finest collection of the kind in the world, and form a spoke of invincible strength in the great wheel of State. Here, in the room set apart for commissions and pardons, you see the great seal of the Union, and in rooms adjoining and above are found the archives of the nation. The diplomatic reception-room is on the floor below, as are also the diplomatic ante-room and the office of the Secretary of State.

In the east wing of the building is the Navy Department, the office of the Secretary of the Navy occupying a position opposite the central stair-cases, which are themselves a beautiful feature of the interior, extending from the basement to the attic. In the corridor you find some superb models of the modern war ships of the United States, and ascending to the fourth floor you visit the Department Library. Other features of this wing are the Hydrographic Office, with its chart printing press, the largest in the United States, and the office of the Nautical Almanac.

The magnificent suite of apartments of the Secretary of War is on the second floor of the west wing, and your visit thereto is repaid by a view of a collection of portraits of the secretaries and distinguished generals.

At the northeast corner of Seventeenth Street and Pennsylvania Avenue you step in at the Corcoran Art Gallery, which, though not a public institution in the sense of being under the patronage of the Government, is one of Washington's most interesting institutions. In its galleries you view an admirable collection of paintings and sculpture, one bit of statuary, Powers' "Greek slave," being in itself worth the visit.

In passing Lafayette Park, on your way to the Treasury Building, you halt for a moment to view the statue of Lafayette and his compatriots, Count de Rochambeau and Chevalier Duportaie, of the French army, and Counts D'Estaing and De Grasse, of the French navy, the work of Antoine Falquiere and Antonin Mercie, and erected in 1890 in pursuance of an order of Congress; and then, finding that the Department of Justice and the

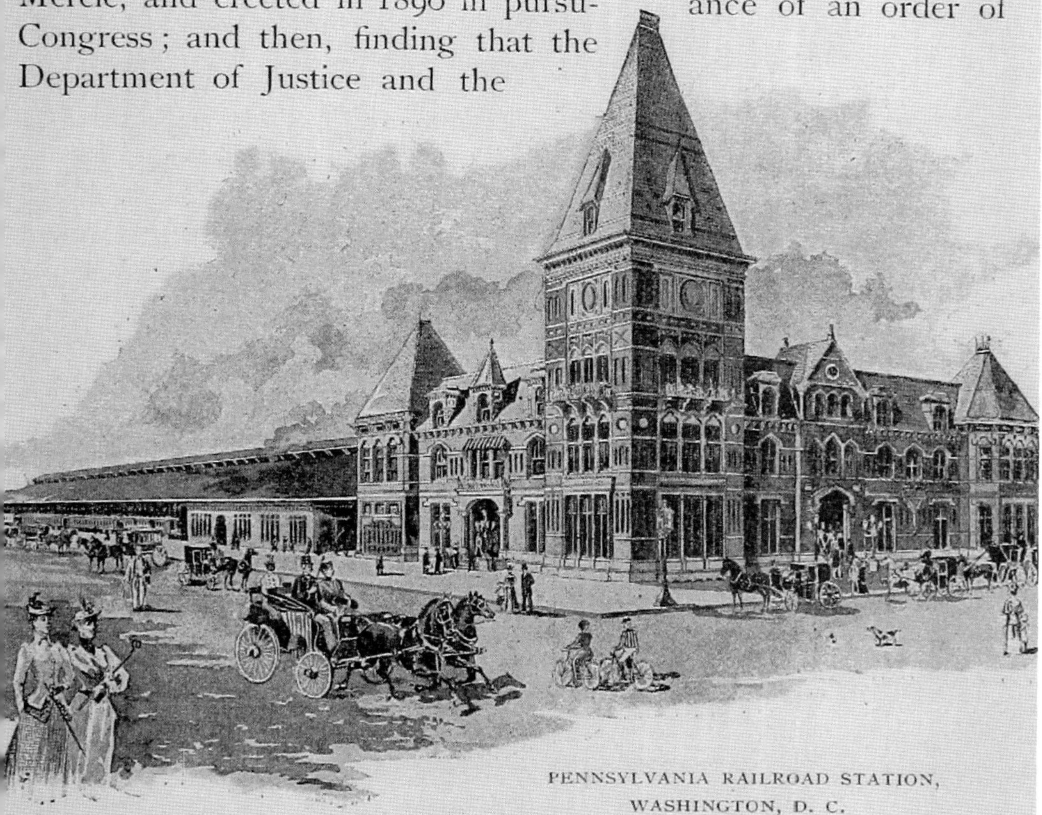

PENNSYLVANIA RAILROAD STATION, WASHINGTON, D. C.

Court of Claims are on your route, you visit both of these.

The enormous building of the Treasury Department has four fronts, the western of which, facing the city, represents the older part of the structure, and is of Virginia freestone, while the other three, built subsequently, are of Maine granite, the monolithic columns of which, on the south front, are among the largest in the world. On entering the building you pass into the cash-room, where all cash disbursements in payment of drafts on the Treasury are made, and at the eastern end of which there is a cash vault for current moneys of the United States, containing something like $40,000,000 at a time. In the basement is the redemption division, where women are engaged in counting, canceling, and destroying notes that have been sent to the Treasury for redemption. In the sub-basement, under the northern court, are the gold and silver vaults. In the office of the Supervising Architect, also in this building, you see the drawings and plans of the public buildings erected in the United States, while on the third floor in the quarters of the Secret Service Division of the Treasury, you come upon not only a collection of photographs of counterfeiters, but a collection of implements used by them as well. The Secretary of the Treasury has his offices on the second floor.

You now proceed to get a view of the south front of the White House by strolling into the President's grounds, where, if it be after half-past five of a Saturday afternoon, you find the Marine Band playing on the lawn. You find, too, on the other side of B Street the United States Fish-Ponds, where carp and other fish are propagated ; you get a better notion of the colossal proportions of the Washington Obelisk than you did from the windows of the East Room ; and you see the forcing houses and nurseries where trees, shrubs, flowers, and foliage plants are propagated by the Government for the ornamentation of its public parks and reservations.

In this vicinity you discover are the Bureau of Engraving and Printing, where you see the process of manufacture of paper money and bonds ; the Department of Agriculture, with its building, its grounds, and its conservatories, in each of which you find something to interest you ; the Smithsonian Institution and National Museum, with their specimens of birds, beasts, fishes, pottery, ceramics, and textiles ; the Army Medical Museum and Library, in which are exhibits of medical supplies, two hundred thousand books on medical subjects, and wax models showing wounds and diseases; and the building of the Fish Commission with its illustrations of fish-hatching and its aquarium.

The department buildings yet to be seen are those of the Interior Department—the Patent Office and the Pension Office—and that of the Post-Office Department. These are located near together, north of Pennsylvania Avenue, and about midway between the Treasury Department and the Capitol. The great granite, freestone, and marble edifice you see covering two blocks between Seventh and Ninth Streets and F and G Streets is the Patent Office, and you revel for hours in its museum of models, which includes every machine or device ever patented in the United States, numbering in all about two hundred thousand. In its superb halls you also find many objects of historic interest, including the original printing press used by Benjamin Franklin.

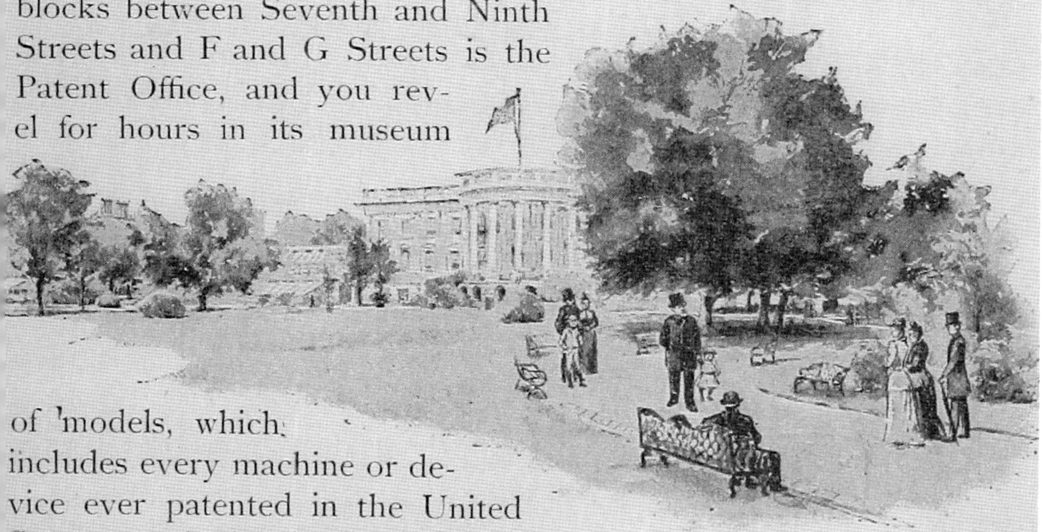

SOUTH FRONT OF THE WHITE HOUSE.

Across the street from the Patent Office, on the south, is the General Post-Office, in which the Postmaster-General has his offices, and on the third floor of which you find some most curiously addressed envelopes and other writings in the Dead Letter Office Museum.

The Pension Office, a few blocks to the east, is the newest of all the public buildings of Washington, and is in strong contrast with the others in point of simplicity as well as in the materials used in its construction, being built of brick, terra cotta, and iron. In this the ball on the occasion of the inauguration of a President is held, and it possesses in its grand court ample accommodation for such a gathering. In its many rooms the business of the Pension Bureau is conducted.

Among the other show-places of the national capital, each and all of which will well repay a visit, are the Naval Observatory at the foot of Twenty-fourth Street, on the banks of the Potomac, where is one of the largest telescopes in the world; the Army Barracks, at the foot of Four and One-half Street, historically interesting because here stands the old Penitentiary, made famous by the prominent part it played in the trials following the assassination of President Lincoln; the Navy Yard and Gun Foundry, which is the chief place in the country for the manufacture of naval supplies, and where you find an interesting museum of naval relics; the Marine Barracks, where, in the armory, concerts are given by the Marine Band; the Congressional Cemetery, where are buried several Congressmen of the early century, two Vice-Presidents—Gerry and Clinton—and generals, admirals, and others of national renown; the United States Jail, where Guiteau, the assassin of President Garfield, was confined and eventually hanged; and the Government Printing Office, wherein are printed the *Congressional Record* and the thousand and one reports, schedules, speeches, and other papers that are deemed worthy of duplication and circulation.

Should you stop in Washington long enough you will devote several days to excursions into the suburbs. You will visit Oak Hill Cemetery in Georgetown, or West Washington, which is one of the most beautiful cities of the dead in the country; you will go out to Arlington, on the Virginia shore of the Potomac, which affords an excellent example of the homestead of an old Virginia family, where you will see the graves of sixteen thousand soldiers who fell in the struggle between the North and the South; and you will take a drive through the most fashionable residence portion of the city and suburbs to the great Falls of the Potomac, where the city reservoir is located, and on which you will see some of the most picturesque scenery around Washington. Mount Vernon, the home of Washington, which remains in all its appointments just as it was when occupied by the Father of his Country, must also be visited, as must the Soldiers' Home and the National Cemetery with its fifty-four hundred and twenty-four graves of soldiers and its granite memorial chapel, in which are the remains of General John A. Logan.

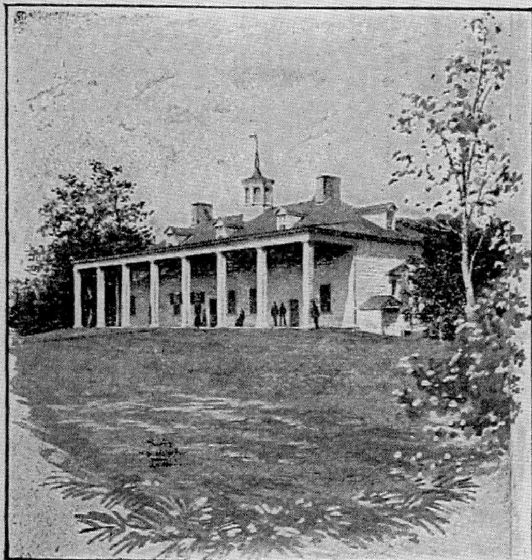

CHICAGO.

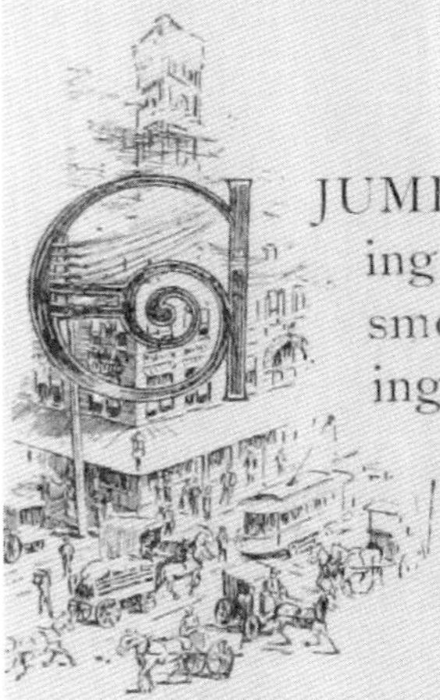

A JUMBLE of vehicles, a murmur of many sounds swelling into a roar, an all-pervading odor of bituminous smoke, a street corner with an iron canopy stretching high above your head across the sidewalk and a row of picturesque buildings opposite. Some one reaches forward for the red ticket with its little punched out holes that you have in your hand; a voice says: "This way, sir!" the open door of an omnibus appears before you, and then you find that you have taken the only vacant seat inside, that the door has closed with a slam, that the horses, answering promptly to the snapping of the driver's long whip, have wheeled sharply to the left, and that your conveyance is picking its way through the riot of wagons, carts, trucks, cabs, and street-cars. Away you go over a narrow iron bridge that is swung across an almost equally narrow stream, and a man on your right tells you that you are crossing the Chicago River, which divides the city into its several sections, and which constitutes an essential part of the city's harbor. Then you plunge into a cañon between huge mountains of stone—a succession of streets overshadowed by mammoth buildings; streets over whose gray, grimy pavements surges the tide of the city's commerce; past the front of the Board of Trade, through the wide doors of which men and boys are swarming as bees swarm in and out of a hive; down this thoroughfare and across that; by great piles of building material out of which new spindling structures are mounting to the smoke-veiled heavens; beside low tumble-down shanties that you fancy must have been built just after the fire of twenty years ago, and that

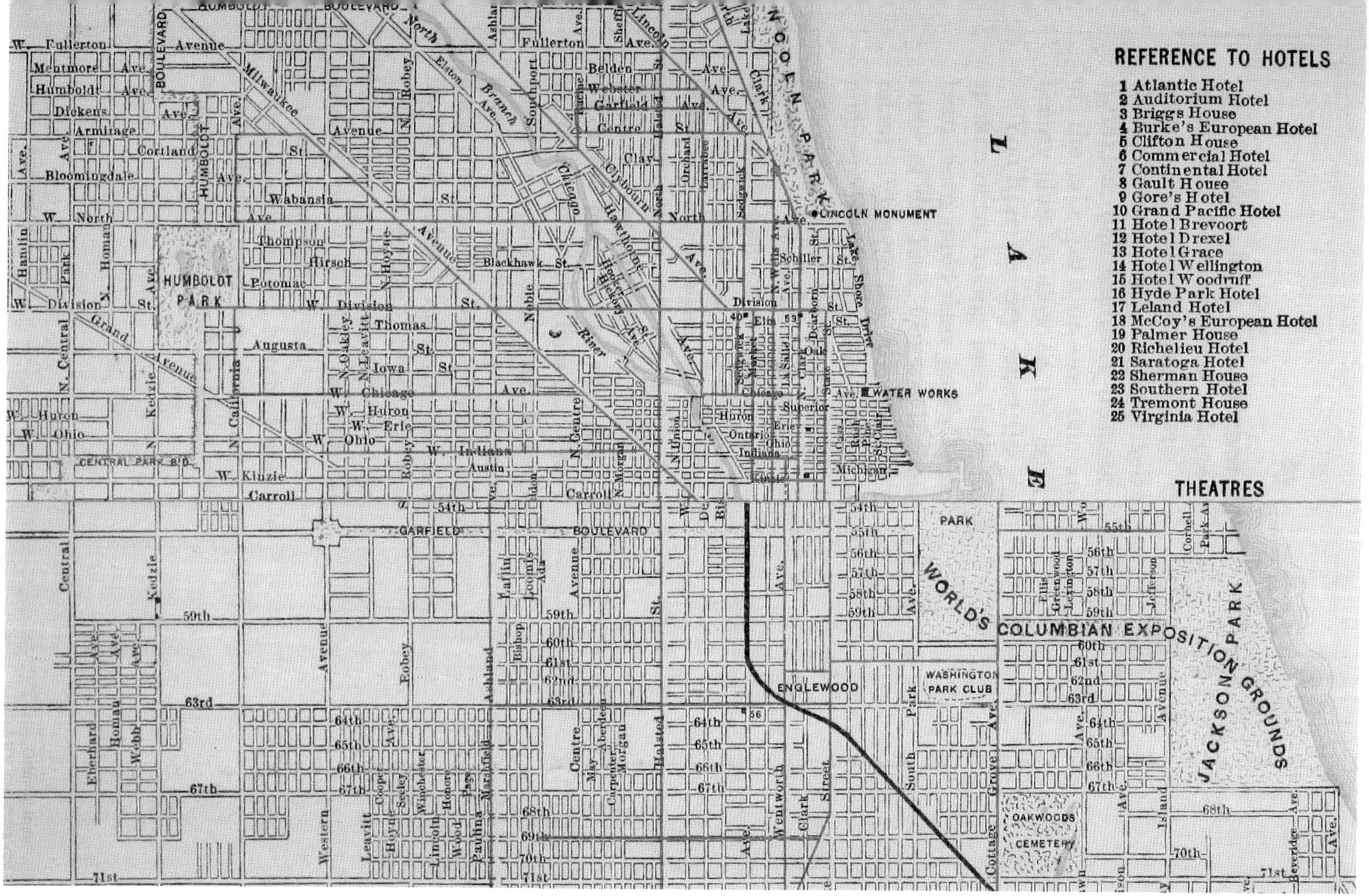
REFERENCE TO HOTELS
1 Atlantic Hotel
2 Auditorium Hotel
3 Briggs House
4 Burke's European Hotel
5 Clifton House
6 Commercial Hotel
7 Continental Hotel
8 Gault House
9 Gore's Hotel
10 Grand Pacific Hotel
11 Hotel Brevoort
12 Hotel Drexel
13 Hotel Grace
14 Hotel Wellington
15 Hotel Woodruff
16 Hyde Park Hotel
17 Leland Hotel
18 McCoy's European Hotel
19 Palmer House
20 Richelieu Hotel
21 Saratoga Hotel
22 Sherman House
23 Southern Hotel
24 Tremont House
25 Virginia Hotel
THEATRES
LAKE
LINCOLN MONUMENT
WATER WORKS
HUMBOLDT PARK
WORLD'S COLUMBIAN EXPOSITION GROUNDS
JACKSON PARK
WASHINGTON PARK CLUB
OAKWOODS CEMETERY
ENGLEWOOD
GARFIELD BOULEVARD
HUMBOLDT BOULEVARD
CENTRAL PARK B'D
Lake Shore Drive

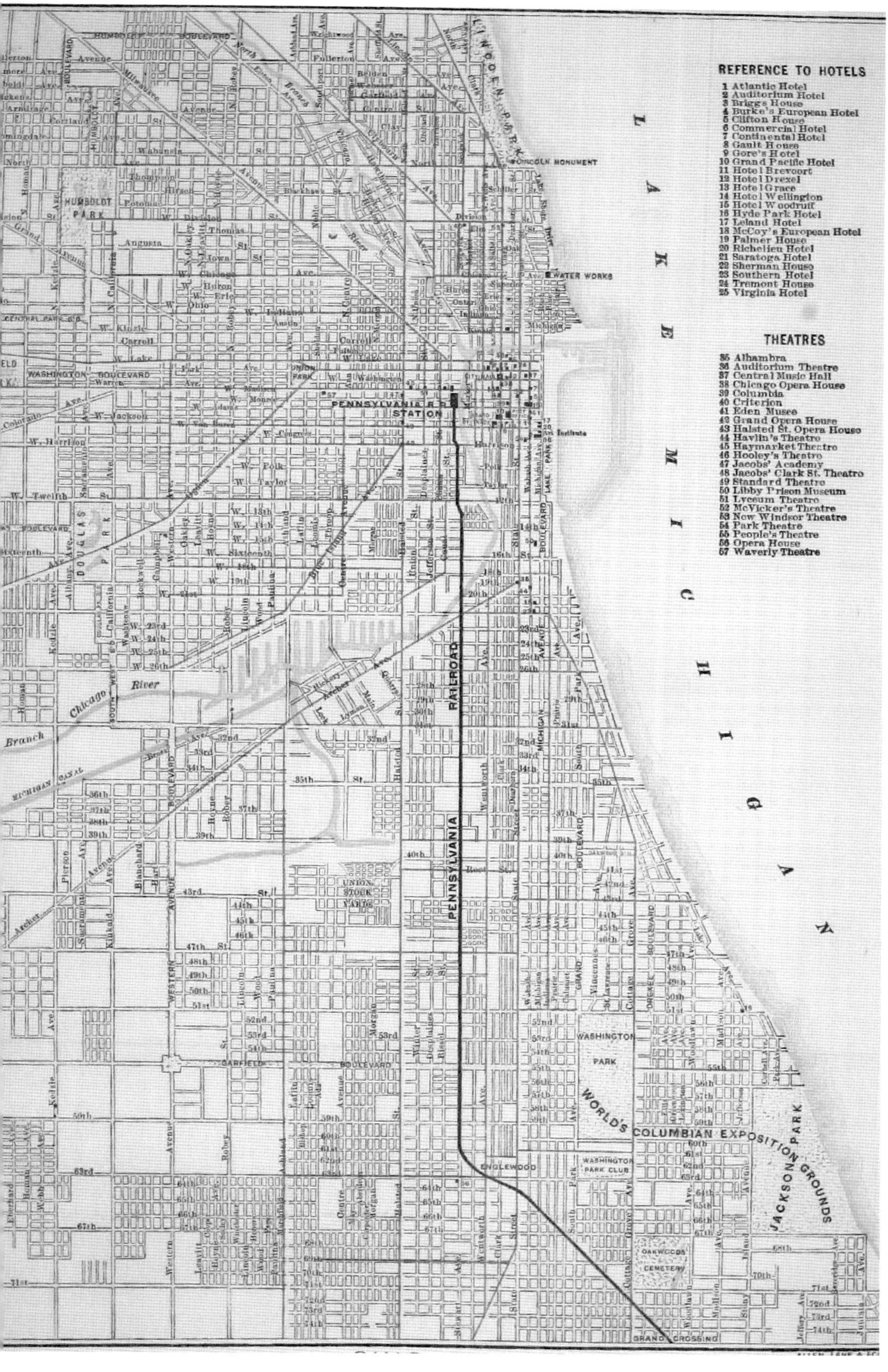
REFERENCE TO HOTELS
1 Atlantic Hotel
2 Auditorium Hotel
3 Briggs House
4 Burke's European Hotel
5 Clifton House
6 Commercial Hotel
7 Continental Hotel
8 Gault House
9 Gore's Hotel
10 Grand Pacific Hotel
11 Hotel Brevoort
12 Hotel Drexel
13 Hotel Grace
14 Hotel Wellington
15 Hotel Woodruff
16 Hyde Park Hotel
17 Leland Hotel
18 McCoy's European Hotel
19 Palmer House
20 Richelieu Hotel
21 Saratoga Hotel
22 Sherman House
23 Southern Hotel
24 Tremont House
25 Virginia Hotel
THEATRES
35 Alhambra
36 Auditorium Theatre
37 Central Music Hall
38 Chicago Opera House
39 Columbia
40 Criterion
41 Eden Musee
42 Grand Opera House
43 Halsted St. Opera House
44 Havlin's Theatre
45 Haymarket Theatre
46 Hooley's Theatre
47 Jacobs' Academy
48 Jacobs' Clark St. Theatre
49 Standard Theatre
50 Libby Prison Museum
51 Lyceum Theatre
52 McVicker's Theatre
53 New Windsor Theatre
54 Park Theatre
55 People's Theatre
56 Opera House
57 Waverly Theatre
LAKE MICHIGAN
LINCOLN PARK
LINCOLN MONUMENT
WATER WORKS
HUMBOLDT PARK
DOUGLAS PARK
UNION PARK
PENNSYLVANIA R.R. STATION
PENNSYLVANIA RAILROAD
UNION STOCK YARDS
Chicago River
MICHIGAN CANAL
WASHINGTON PARK
WORLD'S COLUMBIAN EXPOSITION GROUNDS
JACKSON PARK
WASHINGTON PARK CLUB
OAKWOODS CEMETERY
ENGLEWOOD
GRAND CROSSING

appear not to have been touched since ; and then a sudden flash of light, a luminous sky reflected by and melting into a broad expanse of blue-green waters, cold as steel, and you have emerged upon the lake front and are rolling along a white, well sprinkled, and therefore dustless, boulevard, the verdant sward of the lake park on one side and one marvel of architectural beauty after another on the other.

You hear the city called the eighth wonder of the world, and spoken of as having been built in a day, because its growth has been more rapid than Jack's beanstalk. As compared with the cities of the East, Chicago is a mere infant in arms, but *such* an infant ! Though not incorporated until 1837, when its population numbered only forty-one hundred and seventy souls, and its area was but ten or eleven square miles, it has in the intervening period, in spite of disasters that would have discouraged nine hundred and ninety-nine cities of a thousand, grown until by the last census it was shown to be the second city in the Union and the sixth in the world, with one million ninety-eight thousand five hundred and seventy-six people within its one hundred and eighty-two square miles of territory.

In the great fire of 1871 $200,000,000 worth of property was swept away by the flames. The fire burned for two days and more, sweeping over sixty-five acres every hour, and eating up seven and a half millions every sixty minutes, and yet there is not a Chicagoan living who will not say that the fire was a blessing in disguise. From the ruins of that conflagration rose the Chicago of to-day. Since 1876 fifty-seven thousand buildings have been erected at a cost of $256,000,000, and with a street frontage of two hundred and fifty-six miles ; Chicago has a park system now that is one of the most magnificent in the world, embracing nineteen hundred and seventy-five acres ; her boulevards and drives are unequaled in America ; her commerce amounts to over a billion and a quarter dollars per annum ; every year she handles from $200,000,000 to $300,000,000 worth of live stock ; Chicago is the greatest railroad centre in the world—twenty-six independent lines entering the city ; $190,000,000 are invested in manufacturing establishments, which employ one hundred and seventy-seven thousand hands, to whom $96,000,000 is paid in wages, and whose products reach a value of $528,000,000 ; and the city is, moreover, the greatest maritime port in the United States, the daily arrivals and clearances of vessels exceeding those of New York by nearly fifty per cent.

A train of cable-cars, four long, glides by you with a whirring sound and goes speeding up the long, wide, straight avenue ; another train of equal length, coming the other way, whirls around a curve at the corner on which you are standing, halts for a second to let off a passenger, and disappears down the cross street ; a policeman motions you and the other waiting pedestrians forward, and, raising his baton threateningly, keeps back an all-too-eager expressman who would have run you down without a single compunction of conscience ; a hansom cab dashes by at the officer's back ; a messenger boy, with a cigarette between his lips, stops you midway betwixt cable track and curbstone to request a light from your cigar ; a fakir, endeavoring to sell a patent shoe blacking to a crowd, is telling ancient jokes in order to gain attention ; and three newsboys are fighting over one customer who has signified his intention to buy a newspaper.

You have spent the morning in the streets of Chicago. You have walked up one and down the next, through this and along that, until the high buildings have become familiar and the dime museums, with their host of pictures decorating their fronts, have begun to seem like old friends. You have seen the Chicago business man, pushing, rushing, and driving as though he had this day only in which to put his affairs in order prior to departure for another sphere ; you have seen him on his way to his office an hour or two after dawn, you have watched him as he hurries through his luncheon at mid-day, and you have found him in too much haste to return to his labors to direct you to the City Hall, scarcely a block away. You have seen the Chicago woman in her street garb, looking much like other American women, save perhaps a little larger and a trifle more florid in her

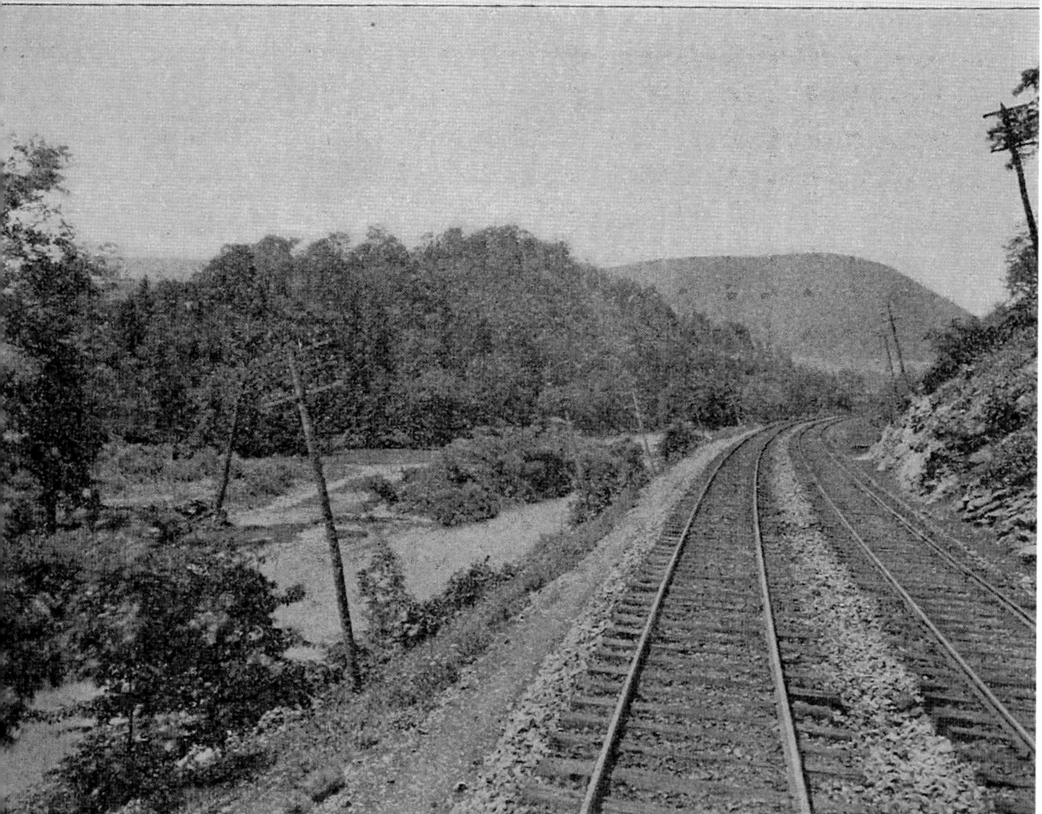

A PICTURESQUE CURVE ON PENNSYLVANIA RAILROAD.

tyle than her Eastern sisters, and you have seen the Chicago rowd, restless, nervous, and surging.

You have found the City Hall yourself at last, and now you re at one of its four corners and are taking in at a glance the randeur of its architectural bulk and detail. It is, you disover, a dual structure that occupies this entire block bounded by

Clark, La Salle, Washington, and Randolph Streets, not only the City Hall, but the County Court-House as well. Its style is that of the modern French renaissance, and its material partly Upper Silurian limestone from Illinois quarries and partly—its columns, pilasters, and medals—of Maine granite.

It is the successor to the old court-house which stood on the same site in the centre of a beautiful green park; and which on that fatal Sunday night in October, 1871, while its bell was still clanging out the dread alarm, took fire from a piece of burning timber, carried by the strong wind for miles, and was totally destroyed. The present building was begun in 1877, upon the ruins of the old one, and was completed five years later, the total cost being something like $5,000,000.

You enter from the Washington Street side the tunnel-like corridor that extends through the entire length of the basement, peep in for a moment at the Health Department, pay a brief visit to the City Detective office, where is located the so-called "sweat-box," where criminals or suspected criminals are subject to the "pumping" process before they are regularly committed, and get an idea of the Chicago police force from the Central District station, and a notion of the fire alarm system in the offices devoted to that department of the municipal service. On the first floor, to which you ascend, you find the offices of the Department of Public Works, police headquarters, and the offices of the mayor of the city. Here, too, the city's finances are kept in order, while on the floor above are found the rooms of the municipal law department and the Board of Education offices. The council chamber, in which the city's sixty-eight aldermen meet and legislate for the people, is on the fourth floor, and there, also, is the public library, with its one hundred and sixty thousand volumes, and its reading-room, which is patronized by about seven hundred thousand people annually.

In the Court-House you are of course chiefly interested in the courts, where you get an impression of American justice as administered in Chicago; but you take time to visit the offices of the sheriff and the coroner, both of whom, being county officers, here have their apartments.

La Salle Street, upon which you emerge, is the money street of the city. All about you are banking institutions, brokerage offices, insurance companies, real estate agencies. A block to the south, as you walk in the direction of the Board of Trade, which seemingly bars the street at its southern extremity, you pass on one corner the Union Building, which includes among its numerous tenants the Western Union Telegraph Company, several banks, and the office of the Western Associated Press; and on the other, the enormous Chamber of Commerce Building, which in many respects is the finest commercial structure in the world and one of the largest office buildings in the country; and from now on one high building after another towers up around you, and you know by instinct that you are in the heart of Chicago. This central business section is one mile square, and is bounded by the lake on one side, the river on two others, and a tremendous system of railways on the fourth. These boundaries, of course, cannot be put back, and if the heart of Chicago is to expand it must expand upward. Into this space every one who has a business desires to get, and these sky-scraping office buildings are the result. It has been suggested that this entire area should be covered with just such buildings as you see around you—buildings from ten to twenty stories in height—and that the streets should be double-decked to afford those doing business or having business in the region a mode of ingress and egress. A simple calculation, however, based on the several buildings of this class already in existence, has shown that if such a plan were to be carried out the number of people employed in the area named would be something like a million and a

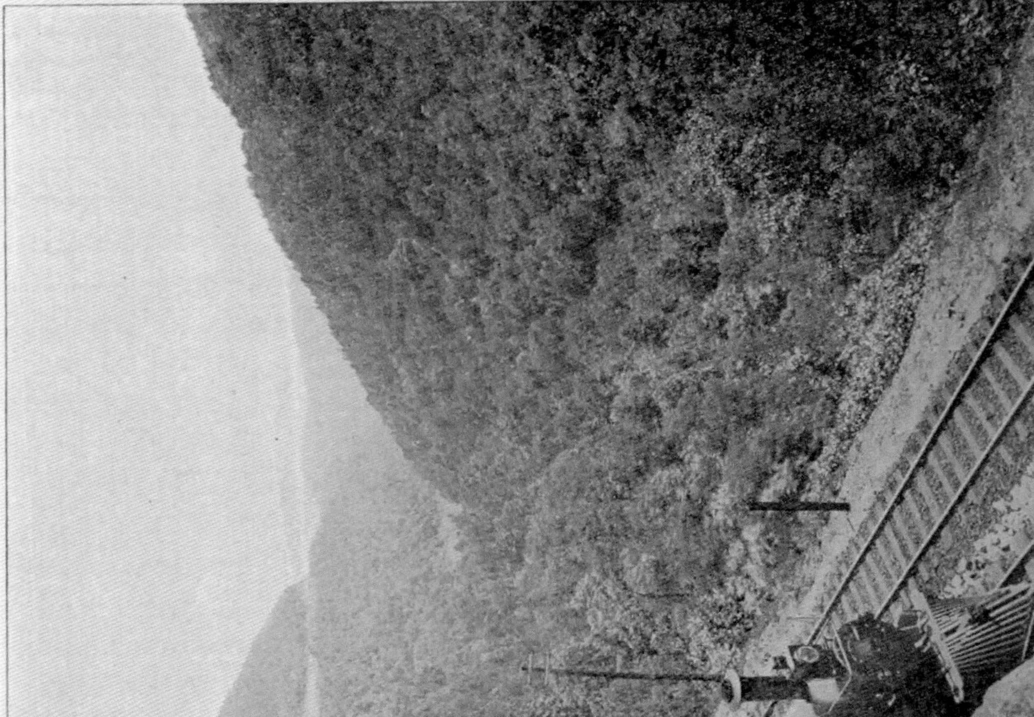

half, and that even with the proposed double-decked streets their coming and going would be an utter impossibility. As it is, between half-past five and half-past six o'clock of an evening the streets in this part of the city are so thronged with the occupants of the big buildings that locomotion is of necessity both slow and laborious.

The Chamber of Commerce Building is divided into five hundred offices; there are an equal number in the Tacoma Building, which mounts to a height that is dizzy to contemplate from the corner of La Salle and Madison Streets; and the Rookery, the most magnificent of all the great office structures, exceeds each of these in accommodations by over one hundred rooms.

"The Rookery," by the way, which you examine with some care, as being typical of the class of buildings you have found dominant in the neighborhood, was erected at a cost of a million and a half of dollars, exclusive of the ground, which belongs to the city, on the site occupied after the fire by the temporary municipal building, a frame structure hastily put up, which immediately began to fall to pieces, and which was given the name of "Rookery" out of contempt for its poor construction, and the crowding necessitated by the inadequacy of its dimensions. The present building has been built and finished in the most expensive fashion throughout. Twelve stories in height, its two lower stories are formed by massive squares of gray granite, whose heavy appearance is somewhat neutralized by the large columns of polished red granite. From the second story up the building is of fire-proof brick and iron.

Near by the Rand-McNally Building, the Insurance Exchange, Maller's Building, the Gaff Building, the Counselman Building, and several other great structures, mounting upward for from ten to twelve stories, and directly before you, as you turn southward once more, is the gray granite building of the Board of Trade, with its swarm of human bees, its graceful tower, and its remarkable weather vane—a lake schooner fifteen feet in length, with rigging in proportion.

Now you climb to the tower and get a bird's-eye view of the city and Lake Michigan, and descending to the street again turn to your right past the Grand Pacific Hotel and visit the Post-Office and Custom-House, which occupy what is locally called the Government Building, a huge structure built on the square bounded by Dearborn, Clark, Adams, and Jackson Streets.

It is not impossible that you have an invitation to dine at the Union League Club, the smoke-begrimed walls of whose building are now in view across the street. In such an event you secure an excellent notion of club life in Chicago, for the reason that the club mentioned is the great general commercial and professional club of the city. It has an active membership of twelve hundred, its revenue is large, and with regard to interior fittings, furnishing, and decorations it possesses the most elegant house in the Western metropolis. You are served with an excellent dinner, and then prior to a proposed visit to some one of the theatres, you inspect the Club Library and Art Gallery, and depart well satisfied that the Chicago man understands the advantages of club comforts as well as business conveniences.

Among the other prominent clubs of Chicago, you are told, are the Chicago Club, the Illinois Club, the Iroquois Club, the University Club, the Marquette Club, the Standard Club, the Calumet Club, the Union Club, and the Press Club.

To make a selection of a theatre in which to spend the evening is not difficult, since Chicago possesses in the Auditorium one of the most spacious and beautiful play-houses in the world. In point of fact it surpasses any theatre in this or any other country in four essential particulars—equipment for stage purposes, interior decorative work, acoustic properties, and the convenience and comfort of its audiences.

Entering from Congress Street you pass through a grand vestibule, with ticket offices on each side, to a mosaic-paved lobby, beneath a low-vaulted ceiling pillared by shapely columns and jetted with electric lights. On your right are several large cloak-rooms, while on your left a broad marble stair-case, protected by solid bronze balusters, rises to the *foyer*. Once within the Auditorium your eyes are greeted with the soft radiance of a harmony in yellow. Walls, ceilings, pillars, and balconies have all been treated in beautiful gradations of the same color, and the whole glows richly beautiful beneath the brilliance of over five thousand electric lights. You count forty boxes hung with delicately tinted plush curtains, and an usher vouchsafes the information that the seating capacity of the house is four thousand and fifty.

The entire Auditorium structure, which fronts on three streets —Michigan Avenue, Congress Street, and Wabash Avenue— includes, beside the theatre in which you are seated, a hotel with four hundred guest-rooms, a business portion with one hundred and thirty-six offices and store-rooms, a recital hall capable of seating five hundred people, and a tower two hundred and twenty-five feet high. Its total cost was $2,000,000, and its weight is one hundred and ten thousand tons.

Among the many other excellent theatres in Chicago, several of which you have passed in your stroll about town during the day, are Hooley's Theatre, where high-class comedy is the rule; the Chicago Opera House, where burlesque is a specialty, and the Grand Opera House, where comic opera usually reigns, which face the City Hall from three different sides; and in the same neighborhood is McVicker's Theatre, on Madison Street, one of the most beautiful play-houses in the United States.

The play over you may get an admirable notion of the society element of Chicago by stopping in for supper at the Auditorium, the Richelieu, or the Wellington, but if you prefer to visit a characteristically Chicago restaurant where well-to-do citizens and their wives eat oysters and drink beer at adjoining tables with variety actors and actresses and other Bohemians, you take a cab to Rector's, at the corner of Monroe and Clark Streets, and descend into that enormous basement with its floors of marble, its walls of white glazed brick, and its many flashing mirrors.

The shops of Chicago you will see, of course, by daylight, and with this object in view you devote yourself for a morning to a stroll north on State Street, which is the longest thoroughfare in the city, and back again to your starting point by way of Clark Street, which, because it penetrates the north division of the city, is regarded as the great north and south artery.

In the shopping district the principal points of interest are the "Leiter" building, extending from Congress Street to Van Buren Street; the "Fair" building, at the corner of State and Adams Streets; and the "Leader," on the opposite side of Adams Street.

At State and Madison Streets you have dry-goods houses on all sides of you. The great dry-goods house of America, however, is that of Marshall, Field & Co., the retail branch of which you discover at the next corner, extending over one-half a square. As for the firm's wholesale department it is something like half a mile away, occupying a whole block, built of granite and sandstone.

If you continue your stroll three blocks farther, passing the Central Music Hall Building, in which is located the College of Music, and the magnificent Masonic Temple, with its twenty stories, you will reach South Water Street with its tangle of wagons, its piles of fruit boxes and chicken crates, and its pyramids of barrels—in other words, the fruit, vegetable, and poultry market of the city.

You return to your starting place by way of Clark Street, which lies two blocks to the west. For the first few squares you remark a great number of drinking saloons, which are to be accounted

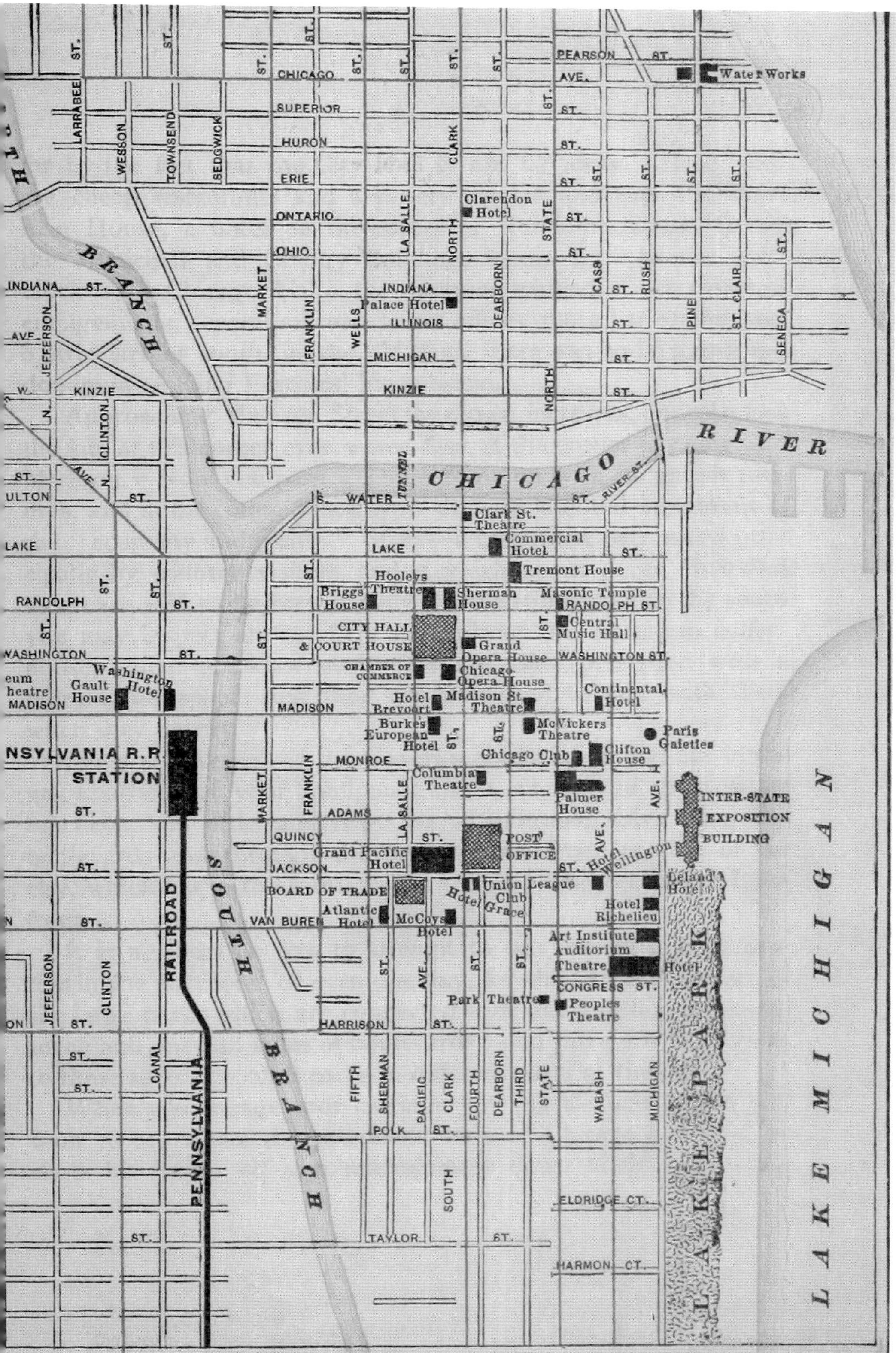

CHICAGO RIVER
NORTH BRANCH
SOUTH BRANCH
LAKE MICHIGAN
LAKE PARK
PENNSYLVANIA R.R. STATION
PENNSYLVANIA RAILROAD
Water Works
Clarendon Hotel
Palace Hotel
Clark St. Theatre
Commercial Hotel
Tremont House
Hooleys Theatre
Briggs House
Sherman House
Masonic Temple
Central Music Hall
CITY HALL & COURT HOUSE
Grand Opera House
CHAMBER OF COMMERCE
Chicago Opera House
Washington Hotel
Gault House
Hotel Brevoort
Madison St. Theatre
Continental Hotel
Burkes European Hotel
McVickers Theatre
Paris Gaieties
Chicago Club
Clifton House
Columbia Theatre
Palmer House
INTER-STATE EXPOSITION BUILDING
Grand Pacific Hotel
POST OFFICE
Hotel Wellington
BOARD OF TRADE
Union League Club
Deland Hotel
Hotel Grace
Atlantic Hotel
McCoys Hotel
Hotel Richelieu
Art Institute
Auditorium Theatre
Hotel
Park Theatre
Peoples Theatre
TUNNEL
PEARSON ST.
CHICAGO AVE.
SUPERIOR
HURON
ERIE
ONTARIO
OHIO
INDIANA ST.
ILLINOIS
MICHIGAN
KINZIE
S. WATER
RIVER ST.
LAKE
RANDOLPH ST.
WASHINGTON ST.
MADISON
MONROE
ADAMS
QUINCY
JACKSON
VAN BUREN
CONGRESS ST.
HARRISON ST.
POLK ST.
TAYLOR ST.
ELDRIDGE CT.
HARMON CT.
LARRABEE ST.
WESSON ST.
TOWNSEND ST.
SEDGWICK
MARKET
FRANKLIN
WELLS
LA SALLE
NORTH CLARK
DEARBORN
NORTH STATE
CASS
RUSH
PINE
ST. CLAIR
SENECA
JEFFERSON
CLINTON
CANAL
FIFTH
SHERMAN
PACIFIC AVE.
CLARK
FOURTH
THIRD
STATE
WABASH
MICHIGAN AVE.
SOUTH

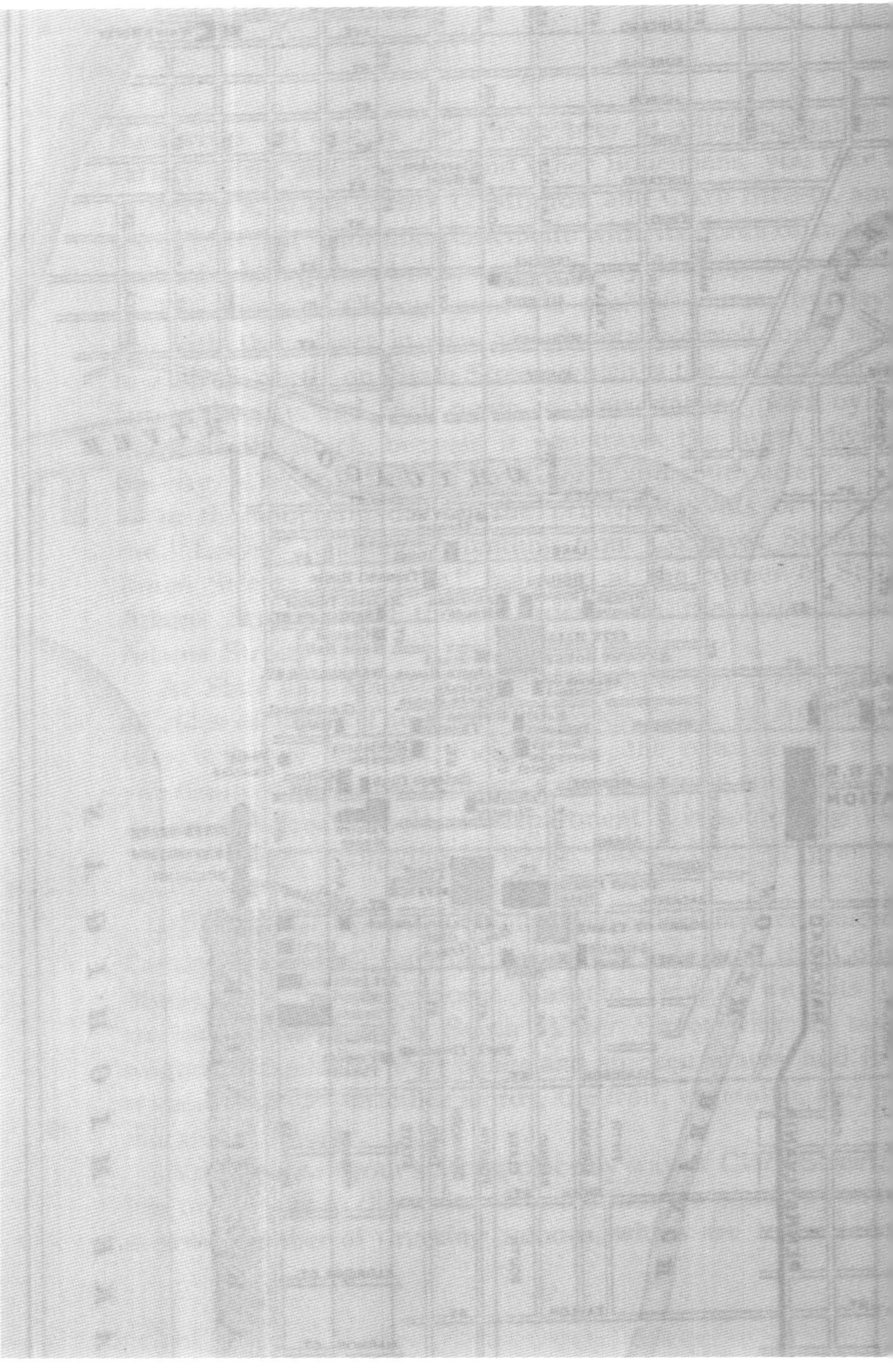

for by the fact that the City Hall is not far away. Here, too, are cheap restaurants and a variety theatre, and then the Sherman House, a hotel on the corner of Randolph Street, facing the Municipal and County Building, looms up. In the next block is the Chicago Rialto, the stamping ground of actors out of engagements, several railroad ticket offices, more bar-rooms, and a little farther south, in the old days, there was to be found the dominion of King Faro and his subjects.

Approaching Madison Street the crowd increases, and you find the jam at this corner even worse than at the corner of State and Madison. Now you pass a Dime Museum with its garish pictures, and in the same block you discover a noted restaurant of the "economy and plenty" order—a restaurant patronized principally by country visitors, and at which about seven thousand meals are said to be served daily; while still farther to the south you may inspect an excellent example of the American coffee-house, where breakfast customers are each presented with a morning newspaper that they are permitted to take with them when they depart.

Now you have passed the Government Building and are in the neighborhood of your hotel once more, where you drop in for luncheon, and order a carriage for an afternoon drive along the boulevards and through the principal residence portion of the city, which lies to the south and in the neighborhood of the Lake front.

It is needless for you to attempt to see the entire Park system in one afternoon, or even one day, for the city is encircled by six large parks which are connected with one another by thirty-seven and one-half miles of boulevards; and there are in addition to these several smaller parks in different parts of the city.

When you engage your carriage you tell the driver that you want to see where the prominent men of Chicago live, and he starts his horses off at a rattling pace down Michigan Avenue to Sixteenth Street. Then he wheels sharply to the left, and after traversing two blocks turns into Prairie Avenue. The probabilities are that you will be disappointed with the street and the dwelling-houses upon it. You have heard, perhaps, that the wealthy men of Chicago live in palaces, and so a great many of them do, but the residents of Prairie Avenue, for the most part, have long ago passed that stage of weakness which demands display. If the exteriors be somewhat lacking in ornamentation, and appear somewhat rusty and time-worn, the interiors are by no means wanting in either comfort or elegance. The walls of many are hung with the works of the greatest masters, and the libraries are libraries in fact as well as name. All this your mentor tells you as you drive along, and as he points out the houses of one millionaire after another. Farther to the south on Calumet Avenue are the homes of other opulent Chicagoans, and the same may be said of the Grand Boulevard and of Michigan Avenue, too, into which you turn for the trip back to your hotel.

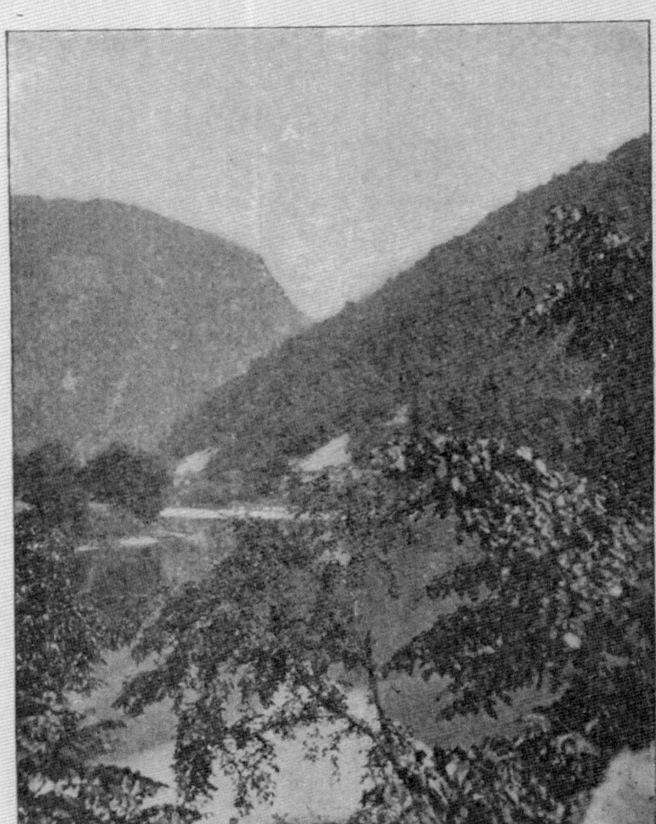

A MOUNTAIN VISTA.

You have, in this drive, been impressed with the extent and the excellent order of the wide boulevards, their firm, dustless, macadamized driveways, their picturesque borders of trees and flowers, and their numerous signs of "No traffic teams allowed," and yet you have had but a mere glimpse of the system, and have not even so much as neared the south parks, where are the buildings of the World's Columbian Exposition.

The Lake Shore drive, which you plan to take in the morning, including a visit to Lincoln Park, the most northern of the public pleasure grounds, is over the grandest boulevard in the city, and past some of its most palatial mansions. This excursion, too, shows you the new sea-wall which is being built out into the lake at an expense that is simply enormous, but which will when completed inclose a long, broad body of lake water available for sailing and rowing, and afford a handsome paved beach, esplanade, and driveway. You may, moreover, if you so desire, stop on your way and inspect the City Water-Works, at the southern end of the Lake Shore drive; and then proceeding to Lincoln Park revel to your heart's content in the many natural and artificial beauties it affords—its undulating lawns, its gracefully winding avenues, its placid lakes, its handsome bridges, its rich floral displays, its zoological gardens, and its monuments and statuary. You return to the city by way of Dearborn Avenue, where you are amazed to find a double row of handsome dwellings stretching for miles, and equaling, if not exceeding, in picturesqueness and variety those that you have already seen.

Your driver, if he takes a friendly interest in you, now suggests that you see the County Jail, in which the Anarchists who incited the riot and threw the dynamite bombs on that fatal night of May 4th, 1886, were confined and hanged; and so on reaching Michigan Street you turn off to the right and stop before the old-fashioned prison, built after the manner of jails constructed in the early years of the present century.

This visit and the chatter with which you are now favored concerning the dynamiters induces you to make another detour when you come to Randolph Street, turning westward to Haymarket Square, where the police monument is erected to the honor of the brave officers who risked or sacrificed their lives in defense of the law, and in commemoration of the death of Anarchy in the city. The scene of the tragedy, in which seven policemen were killed outright or died shortly after as a result of their wounds, is pointed out to you on Desplaines Street, between the Haymarket and an alley running east, and you look with some degree of awe upon the street in front of Crane Brothers' manufactory, where stood the wagon from which the Anarchist speakers addressed the mob, and near which the terrible explosion occurred.

One of the greatest show-places in the city you have yet to visit. Chicago is a great manufacturing city, and a great commercial city, but its greatest industry is its live stock business, and to see Chicago and not see the Union Stock Yards is to see the play of "Hamlet" with *Hamlet* left out. So you put on some old clothes and take a State Street cable-car going south, and transfer at Forty-third Street to a car going west. At the entrance to the yards, which cover a tract of over four hundred acres, you gladly avail yourself of the proffered services of a guide, who conducts you throughout the vast inclosure, explaining everything as you go. "The plant of the Union Stock Yards Company," he tells you, "cost $4,000,000, and the various packing companies having buildings in the vicinity have invested in their business something like $17,000,000 additional. The number of *employés* at the yards is twenty-four thousand five hundred, and the yards' greatest capacity is twenty thousand head of cattle, twelve thousand hogs, and fifteen thousand head of sheep. There are here twenty miles of wood-paved streets, twenty miles of drinking troughs supplied with fresh water from six artesian wells, and fifty miles of feeding troughs."

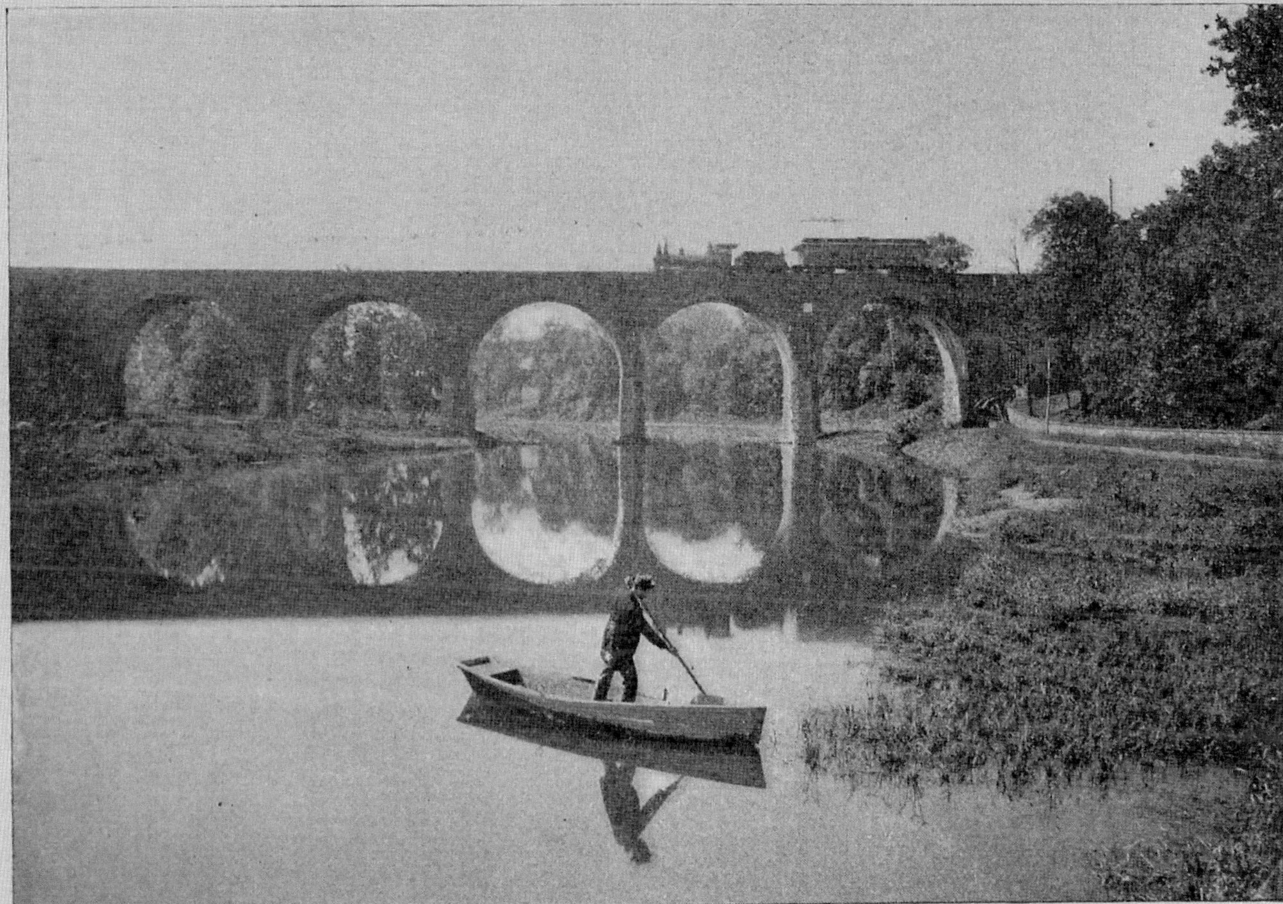

PICTURESQUE SCENE FROM THE CAR WINDOW.

You watch with interest the process of turning a live bullock into so much beef, and are surprised not a little at the way in which the labor is divided, the rapidity with which the transformation is accomplished, and the careful manner in which every part of the beast is utilized for one purpose or another. You see the swine driven in and weighed, you see it killed, bled, and scalded, and its bristles shaved off and preserved, and you see it quartered, the hams and shoulders going one way and the sides into a pickle bath. So, too, you see the sheep changed into mutton, and you turn away wondering at the appetite of the world that consumes all this meat and more daily.

You have now received a fairly good idea of the city and its principal points of interest, but there still remain many other features that, if you have the time to spare, you may visit with profit. You may, for instance, run out to the town of Pullman, ten miles south of the city, on the shore of Lake Calumet, which, founded by George M. Pullman, the palace-car magnate, realizes, in some respects, the supreme idea of socialism, though no community probably is more unsatisfactory to the socialistic dreamer. Primarily it is the home of the extensive car-works of the Pullman Palace Car Company, which have a capacity of about $10,000,000 worth of cars per annum, about fifty passenger, freight, and street cars being completed daily ; but there are in the town, you will find, many other objects worth seeing.

So, too, in Chicago itself there are other points that a month's visit would fail to exhaust—the manufactories, the libraries, the Art Institute, the charitable institutions, the House of Correction, the Fire Department, the schools and colleges, the museums, the cycloramas, the railroad depots, the bridges, the tunnels, the viaducts, the wharves, the street-car system, the elevated railroads, the banks and clearing-houses, the relics of old Chicago when it was but a swamp between prairie and lake, the fire relics, and a host of other matters and things that the city can alone suggest,

THE WORLD'S COLUMBIAN EXPOSITION OF 1893.

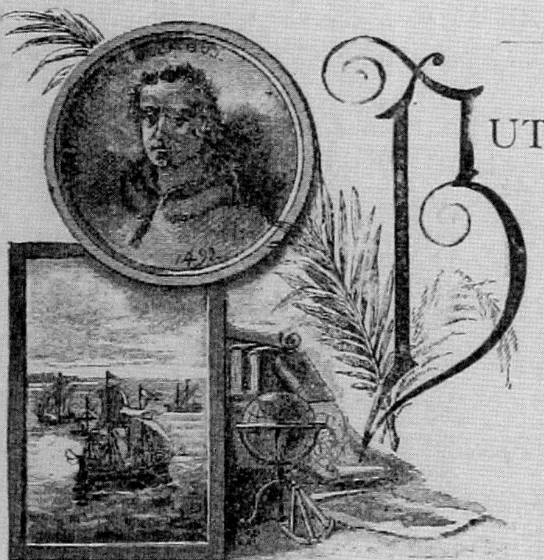

BUT one and a half years ago two-thirds of Jackson Park was a wilderness—two or three small groves of scrub oak and maple, with here and there a clump of fiery sumac alone breaking the dreary waste of swamp land. When, in May, 1893, the President of the United States shall proclaim the Columbian Exposition open, these same broad acres on the shore of Lake Michigan will bear upon their breast a city more beautiful than artist's brush ever dared to picture or poet's fancy to sing—a city whose pinnacles will pierce the clouds and whose glistening domes will rival in dazzling glory the effulgence of the sun itself; a city that will teem with treasures gathered from the four corners of the earth; a city in which the wonders of the age will be grouped in alluring yet embarrassing profusion; a city in whose harbor will be gathered the marine craft of four centuries, and through whose streets will saunter visitors from every clime.

You stand upon the huge pier jutting far out into the lake and gaze about you. The transformation is now complete. It is the spring of 1893. The last nail has been driven, the last exhibit has been put in place, the great gates have been flung wide, and the World's Columbian Exposition is an accomplished fact. From this coign of vantage you get your first view of what has been prepared for you. Hitherto you have been told a good deal about the Fair in a general way. You know, for instance, that it extends over not only Jackson Park, with its five hundred and eighty-six acres, but that Washington Park, a mile away, with its three hundred and seventy-one acres, and the connecting strip of land, eighty acres in extent, called Midway Plaisance, have also been utilized to a greater or less extent, and you realize how much more stupendous it must be than the Paris Exposition of 1889, which, with the Champ de Mars, the Trocadero, the Esplanade des Invalides, and the quays, took in but one hundred and seventy-three acres in all. You remember, too, that the principal buildings here cover one hundred and fifty acres, while those at Paris covered but fifty-five, and you are consequently prepared, in a measure, for the spectacle which rises up before you as you look across the crystal surface of the breakwater-protected harbor, with its many and varied craft, to the gracefully curving shore line and the magnificent group of buildings beyond.

To your right, and by far the most conspicuous object from the lake, is the long, high, yet thoroughly symmetrical structure of the Manufactures and Liberal Arts Building, its extraordinary length broken midway by a lofty arched entrance between elaborately ornamented piers and surmounted by bright-hued banners that seem, so high are they, to be fluttering among the clouds, while higher still above it all rises the domed roof of glass reflecting the blue of the heavens. Along its whole extent, too, at intervals, upon the green lawns that slope from its ivory-colored walls to the white stone esplanade that skirts the lake, you notice picturesque little cafés with gaudy awnings, and beyond, before the turreted structure from which the stars and stripes are flying, and which you know must be the building of the United States Government, you get a long-distance view of blue-uniformed troops going through a series of evolutions upon the parade ground in front of an encampment of snowy tents; while just off shore here, as if to contrast the navy with the army, you discover the white hull, spindling mast, and short smoke stacks of a line of battle ships.

Directly before you, across a broad colonnade, beneath which a high and wide arch gives free access from the harbor to the canal system of the grounds, and along which, equidistantly spaced, are forty-eight symbol-capped columns representative of the forty-eight States and Territories of the Union, is the grand avenue with its broad, gondola-flecked basin, from whose mirror-like surface rises St. Gauden's colossal statue of "Liberty." Fountains are throwing aloft a myriad jets that glitter in the sunlight like so many endless ropes of dazzling gems, and on either side the beautiful facades of the Liberal Arts and the Agricultural Buildings face each other from the top of terraces that gradually slope to the dividing waters. At the far end of the basin, flanked by the Machinery Hall on one side and the Electrical and Mining Buildings on the other, you descry the blazing domes of the Administration Building, and even at this distance you concede the good judgment of those who predicted that this, of all the structures on the grounds, would be the crowning triumph of the Exposition.

The colonnade, across which this view is presented, and which, in its general features, reminds you of that leading to St. Peter's, at Rome, connects, you now observe, two buildings, and from the one at the north, even as you begin to admire its shapely outline, there floats out to you across the harbor the music of many voices. It is the Music Hall of the Fair, and a Musical Congress is holding daily sessions within its spacious walls. The building to the south, a guard tells you, serves as a restaurant, while as for the curious little structure on that tongue of rising ground, projecting into the lake, at this restaurant's southeastern corner, it is an exact copy of the Convent of La Rabida, at Palos, in which Columbus lived while perfecting his plans for his voyage of discovery,

Recalled thus to a realization of the event that the Exposition celebrates, and remembering that among the features of the naval pageant recently held in New York Harbor were models of the caravel *Santa Maria*, and her consorts *Pinta* and *Nina*, the fleet with which Columbus crossed the Atlantic, you search among the many curious and incongruous vessels anchored or drifting in the harbor for these copies of the Spanish cruisers of 1492, to find them, it is likely, appropriately moored under the shadow of the convent walls.

And now a steamboat, crowded to the guards, is being made fast to the pier ; a throng of visitors rushes down the gang-plank and you join in the procession that hurries shoreward. Thus far you have got a very general idea of the Exposition—a notion merely of some of the greater buildings and their location. The picture was beautiful, but it was, to a certain extent, misleading. You have not as yet seen a tithe of the whole show, and what you have seen has been dwarfed by the distance from which you viewed it. Once on shore you turn to your left, pass between the restaurant building, that you saw from the pier, and the convent building, in which are no end of relics of the Spanish discoverer, and mounting a stairway to the elevated railroad and moving sidewalk, take passage upon the latter for a tour of the grounds. The moving sidewalk, which at an elevation traverses the length and breadth of the Jackson Park portion of the Exposition, is an exhibit of the cable-car companies of the city, the motive power being an endless cable worked by powerful engines. A moving platform or sidewalk is running at the rate of three miles an hour, and adjoining this, so that you may without danger step from the one to the other, is a similar platform furnished with a succession of benches and making a speed of six miles an hour. Seated on one of these benches you are now passing between the Agricultural Annex, with its overflow exhibits of agricultural machinery, and the Forestry Building, devoted to the purpose which its name indicates. On your left are the extensive live stock sheds covering no less than forty acres, and on your right, as you circle around the southern end of the grounds proper, running now side by side with a fast flying train of the electrical elevated railroad, is the circular inclosure used for a cattle exhibit and connecting with the colonnade that joins the Agricultural Building with Machinery Hall. Now you skirt the rear of this latter-named building with its boiler-houses and steam-generating plant, dart in between it and its chief annex on the west, and are carried over the sheds into which run the tracks of the score or more of railroads having a terminus at the grounds.

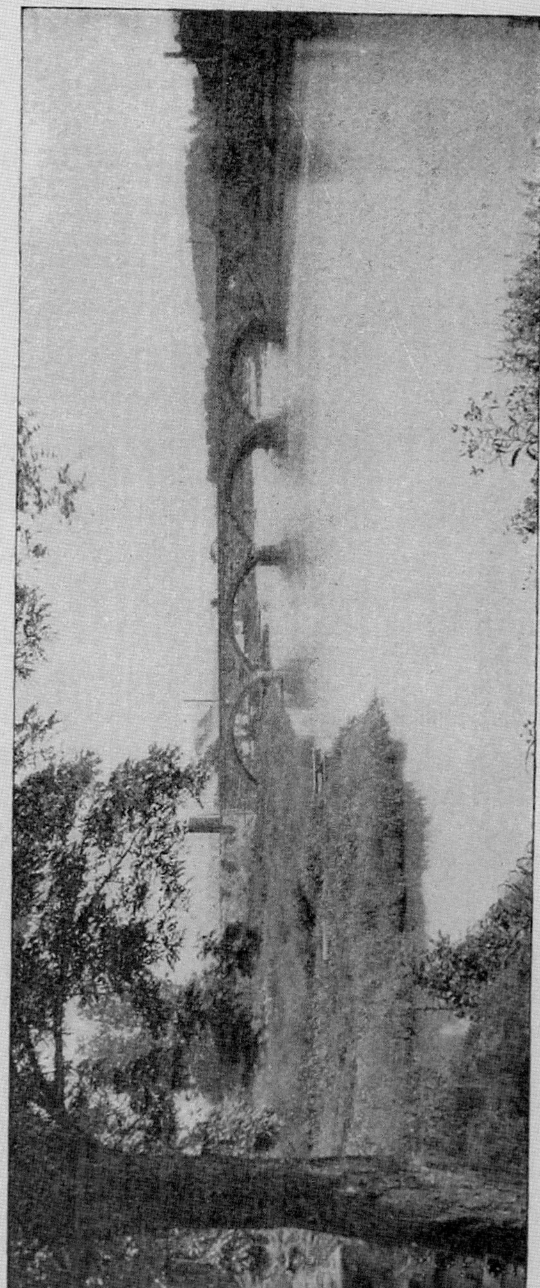

The view on your right, with the Administration Building directly before you, and the Grand Avenue with its splendid facades stretching away on either side of the grand canal to the lake, is one of the most beautiful prospects afforded by the trip, and gives you a very much more adequate idea of this the chief point of the Exposition than was afforded by the view you had of it in the opposite direction.

Curving to the westward at the southwest corner of the Mines and Mining Building you pass the southern end of the richly-colored Transportation Building, decorated in gold, yellow, and red, the national colors of Spain, in commemoration of the fact that it was that country that provided the first means of transport to the New World. You traverse the western front of this structure, and then at a little distance pass Horticultural Hall, with its rose-tinted walls and its dome of glinting glass. The smaller building, which next appears on your right, looking for all the world like a Pompeiian palace, its marble-like sides a warm ivory, deepening into orange, and its roof a brilliant red, is that devoted to woman's work, while off to your left, along what is called the Midway Plaisance, you see the quaint towers, arches, and minarets of a group of structures distinctively foreign—the bazaars of all nations and a various collection of attractions of a semi-private character.

Approaching now the northern end of the Fair grounds you pass in rapid succession the pavilions of some of the Western States and Territories, and turning eastward once again find still more of these architecturally-ornamented State reservations. For some distance you follow the Lake Shore southward, flit by one of the annexes of the Art Gallery, getting a glimpse of the turquoise dome of the Art Palace itself, and alight, finally, between the Aztec temple, erected by the Republic of Mexico, and one of the arms of the lagoon system, having traveled about three miles from your starting point.

In order to get an idea now of the water-ways of the grounds you descend a broad sweep of stone steps between flower-garnished terraces to a spacious landing stage, where you engage one of the many rapid-moving electric launches to convey you through the lagoons and canals to the great basin. Comfortably reclining on a cushioned seat in the stern, and shielded from the sun's rays by an ample awning, you float swiftly over the surface of the clear, sparkling waters, passing dozens of boats like your own, sombre-looking gondolas propelled by Venetian-like gondoliers, row-boats, steam launches, and canoes, all filled with jolly, gleeful folk like yourself, out for a holiday and apparently enjoying every moment to the full. The terraced shores, too, are crowded with sight-seers, and there on the wide plateau to your left are the encamped soldiers indulging in a grand review by the commander-in-chief of the army, and in the presence of thousands of spectators. Now you glide between the Government Building on one hand and the Fisheries Building on the other, and shooting beneath the wide span of a picturesque bridge find yourself on the principal lagoon to the east of a beautiful wooded island, from whose fertile soil rises specimens of a thousand trees indigenous to the United States, richly blooming azalias, gorgeous rhododendrons, and scores of other flowering and decorative shrubs ; aquatic fowls of every clime are swimming about you, darting here and there, or taking wing and flying off to the verdant shores of the leafy isle, and your sportsman's instincts assert themselves only to be vigorously repressed as a flock of fat widgeon get up in front of your boat and circle off into one of the less frequented bays. A little farther on you see a white sea-gull, and before you have passed half the length of the Liberal Arts structure, along whose western side you are now skimming, your watchful gaze has been rewarded with sight of several swans, a brown pelican, a stork, a couple of scarlet ibes, and a flamingo. The Main Building is still shutting off your view lakeward even after you have shot under another bridge and have come in sight of the Electrical Building on your left, and it continues to do so until at length you float out into the Grand Canal.

Your landing is made in front of the Main Building's southern facade, and as you join the crowd ascending the broad flight of snowy steps to the grand avenue you realize for the first time the grandeur of this mammoth palace. In coloring it has the tone of old alabaster, the surface of which has begun to disintegrate, and so closely does the "staff" or stucco, of which its panels and columns are composed, resemble this material that you can scarcely believe it a less substantial imitation. About the great arched middle entrance you observe a wealth of sculptured adornment, in which female figures symbolical of the various arts and sciences play a conspicuous and attractive part, while medallions representative of the arms and seals of the several States, and of foreign nations as well, find employment in ornamenting both architrave and spandrel. Once inside the building you are still further impressed by its vastness, and you are not surprised to learn that to make a complete circuit of it means to travel a full mile, and that so high is its great arched roof that the entire Auditorium Building, of which Chicago is so justly proud, tower and all, could be wheeled beneath it. You observe that above a certain point no attempt has been made to decorate the space overhead, save to paint it a light tone that at night reflects the electric light ; but the long lines of gallery front have been treated with a good deal of modeled work sufficiently strong in color to give animation, while broad gold and colored bands ornament the lower portion of the roof. There are three side-galleries, you discover, inclosing the great central gallery, while between the enormous girders of the central roof other galleries have been placed twenty-five feet above the ground and projecting into the hall, from which you get a general view of the immense array of exhibits and the busy scene on the floor below.

But it is not merely a general view that you desire, and so descending to the fifty-foot wide avenue, that has been named "Columbia," and that extends through the entire length of the building, you begin an examination of the million interesting objects there on exhibition. Passing from the section set apart for one nation to that of another, and from one group of exhibits to an entirely different group, you soon find yourself experiencing a veritable night-mare, in which paints and varnishes, type-writers and stationery, upholstery goods and wall papers, tiles and pottery, metal work and stained glass, gold and silver ware, watches and clocks, silks and woolens, furs and laces, rubber goods and leather goods, cook stoves and refrigerators, iron gates and cutlery, are jumbled in inextricable confusion.

Now you dart off into the department set aside for the Liberal Arts, including education, literature, engineering, music, and the drama, and find relief for the time being from the embarrassing richness of the manufactures. But the most interesting display within this mammoth inclosure you have yet to see, and that is the Ethnological Museum, which is in charge of Professor F. W. Putnam, of Harvard College.

The most important part of the collection, you observe, refers to North and South America. Commencing with the earliest traces of the existence of man in the Northern Hemisphere, illustrations are shown of the geology, the flora, and the fauna of the period, the latter including actual specimens of the mammoth and the mastodon. Here, too, you see models of the great earth-works in Ohio, in which are combined squares, octagons, circles, and other figures, and, what particularly interests you, the massive skeleton of a man encased in copper armor, the head covered by an oval-shaped copper cap, and the neck encircled by a necklace of bears' teeth set with pearls, together with a similar female skeleton. These, you learn, were recently discovered in one of the Ohio mounds fourteen feet below the surface of the earth, and are generally supposed to be the skeletons of the King and Queen of the Mound Builders, and to have been buried fully six hundred years ago.

Another class of exhibits in this same collection includes the ancient cliff houses and ruined pueblos of Colorado, Arizona, and New Mexico; models of the existing pueblos, such as those of Moki and Zuni, which appear to form a direct link with the past races; and reproductions of some portion of those great stone buildings in Central America, Mexico, and Peru of which there is but little knowledge. Here, too, you see many groups of natives from different tribes not only of North and South America, but from Europe, Asia, and Africa as well, including several pygmies from the land of Tippu-Tib, living in their own huts and engaged in their own special industries. A number of these little colonies, however, you find not in the main building at all, but outside in the open air, some of the principal ones being a part of the Indian Bureau exhibit, and consequently located near the Government Building. Here the Navajos are weaving blankets, the Zunis, dwelling in what they call a "hogan," are making pottery, while the Piutes are fashioning water-bottles out of rushes.

On your return journey through this tremendous store-house of manufactures and liberal art works you discover many things that you overlooked in your scurry northward, stopping perhaps to inspect with some degree of care the exhibit of a Kansas taxidermist, which includes one hundred and fifty of the largest animals of the United States—buffalo, elk, moose, antelope, deer, mountain sheep, goats, wild cats, wolves, and bear—or the American Sportsman's Exhibit, comprising every weapon and utensil used in hunting, fishing, and trapping from the time the country was discovered to the present day.

Then, coming out at the southeastern corner beneath another of the buildings' elaborately ornamented archways, you pass along the colonnade that bridges the great basin, and approach the Agricultural Building, getting as you go an excellent view of this single-story structure, with its imposing main entrance between colossal Ionic columns, its statuary-ornamented roof, its mammoth glass dome in the centre, and its lesser domes at the corners, each surmounted by three female figures of herculean proportions supporting an enormous globe. The tremendous structure you have just left covers thirty and a half acres, and the one you are now about to enter seems small in comparison with its nine acres only of floor space. Passing in at the main portal, which is designed as a temple to Ceres, with a statue of the goddess in the centre, rising from a mosaic floor of black and white to indicate the Ionic character of the building, and surrounded by a lofty colonnade and domed roof all richly expressed in gold and color, you find yourself in one of a large number of small galleries that surround the central rotunda, which is one hundred feet in diameter and one hundred and thirty feet high.

Every inch of ground space, outside the wide avenues and the arcade which runs all the way around the building, is devoted to exhibits of a somewhat prosaic character. Here, for example, you travel in and out among great piles of biscuits, cakes, and crackers, and a little farther on come upon pyramids of cans of preserved fruits and meats, while a large portion of the building, you soon discover, is taken up with farming tools, implements, and machinery. These have, it is true, been grouped and arranged with an eye for picturesque effect, but unless you are especially interested in the subject you are willing to make your stay in the agricultural palace a brief one. As a consequence, you grasp as well as you can its chief architectural features, and then make your escape by way of the colonnade which connects its southwestern extremity with Machinery Hall, stopping *en route* to visit the live stock Assembly Hall, which is just south of the colonnade. Here on the first floor is the Bureau of Information and the offices of scores of cattle and horse associations, dog and pet stock associations, and other live stock organizations; while on the floor above is an assembly hall in which you find a body of grangers listening to an address on some topic connected with their field of work.

If you are particularly interested in agriculture you will be interested in forestry and dairy products as well, and will turn eastward instead of westward, and visit the buildings devoted to these purposes, which lie between the Agricultural Annex and the lake ; and you will stop for an hour or two, perhaps, also to look at the live stock display—the horses, the cattle, the swine, and the sheep that will be found beneath the sheds to the south of the other structures.

Whether you care for these things or not, however, you will surely drop in at this quaintly picturesque Spanish house that overlooks the lake, and that you now recognize as the copy of the Convent of La Rabida that you saw first from the pier, and afterwards as you passed up to the elevated moving sidewalk. Inside you find a store-house of relics. Beginning with maps, models, and *fac-similes* illustrating the condition of navigation and the knowledge of geography before and during the time of Columbus, there is likewise exhibited a statue of Leif Erikson, together with maps and charts of his alleged voyages, and the settlement that it is claimed he made in Greenland years before Columbus sighted the West Indies. The Norse ships of this period are also shown by means of models, as well as a fine collection of old navigating and other nautical instruments. In another room you discover the life history of Columbus, illustrated by views of the various cities that claim him as their son, models of the houses in which he was supposed to have been born ; photographs of the University of Pavia, where he was educated, &c., &c. In still another room you come across an extensive picture gallery, including all the paintings, either originals or copies, in which Columbus figures, while in yet another apartment are the portraits, busts, and statues of Columbus.

Machinery Hall, which you next visit, presents but a poor prospect from the south, and so you approach it by way of the Grand Avenue, crossing the bridge between it and Machinery Hall, and getting an excellent prospective from its northeast corner. Though lacking the boldness that makes of the Administration Building the architectural *chef-d'œuvre* of the Exposition, this edifice impresses you as more artistically pleasing than either its gigantic neighbor devoted to manufactures and the liberal arts, or its equal-sized sister across the lagoon devoted to agriculture. In its details it suggests sunny Seville, though the general character of the architecture, like that of the other buildings fronting on the Grand Avenue, is thoroughly classic. Composed of three long arch-roofed compartments, similar to trainsheds—the idea being to dispose of them at the close of the Exposition for that purpose—the ornamentation is devoted entirely to the exterior, which is rich with columns and arches opening to an inner arcade, domed and turreted corner pavilions and statue-adorned towers rising from either side of the imposing porticos that form the main entrances.

Here you see machinery of all kinds in motion. There are motors for the generation and apparatus for the transmission of power ; hydraulic and pneumatic devices ; fire-engines and fire-ladders ; machines for working metals and machines for working stone ; machines for twisting silk and machines for weaving fabrics ; type-setting machines and printing presses ; paper-making machinery ; wood-working machinery ; glass-cutting machinery ; pumps, elevators, and a thousand and one odd patented arrangements that you have never so much as dreamed of.

And then, back of all this, in another building—the Machinery Annex—off to the west, covering between four and five acres, is almost as much again of the same sort ; while to the south, connected with the main structure, is what is known as the boiler plant, which supplies steam to the great power station which occupies a space along the entire south side of this great storehouse of mechanism. Here you find engine after engine of all makes and all sizes, from the comparatively small affair of one hundred and fifty horse-power to the enormous machine of one thousand horse-power, aggregating fully twenty-five thousand horse-power in all. From this source, you learn, power is furnished not alone to Machinery Hall, but throughout the grounds to the various other buildings, supplying them with light and heat, as well as affording energy for other purposes. It is not steam, though, that is sent through the tunnels, but compressed air, which is used to operate all the machinery in motion.

The Administration Building, which next claims your attention, is well worth a careful study from without as well as from within. Viewed from the elevation of your moving sidewalk ride about the grounds, the great ovoid dome, two hundred and twenty feet in height, has appeared to you somewhat out of proportion to the underlying foundation, but now as you stand on the pavement of the Grand Avenue and gaze up at it, you realize that a dome of less girth and amplitude would have looked meagre and ineffectual. The general design of the building, which is two hundred and fifty feet square, is, you observe, in the style of the French renaissance. The first great story, of the Doric order, is of heroic proportions, surrounded by a lofty balustrade and having the great tiers of the angle of each of the four pavilions which form its corners crowned with sculpture. The second story, with its lofty and spacious colonnade, is of the Ionic order. The design, you notice, has been divided in its height into three principal stages. The first, consisting of the four pavilions, corresponding in height with the various buildings grouped about it, which are about sixty-five feet high ; the second stage of the same height, a continuation of the central rotunda ; and the third stage, the base of the great dome, thirty feet in height and octagonal in form, and the great dome itself, which is over one-third the height of the entire structure.

On the panels of the first story are inscriptions detailing facts in the life of Columbus, and the names of discoverers of continents or portions of continents, and when you have entered by one of the fifty-feet wide, deeply recessed, and semi-circular arched portals, you find upon the interior still more inscriptions recording important discoveries in science and the names of the discoverers.

The interior features of the building approach, if they do not exceed, in beauty and splendor those of the exterior. Between every two of the grand entrances and connecting the intervening pavilion with the great rotunda you find a hall or loggia thirty feet square giving access to the offices, and provided with broad circular stairways and swift-running elevators. In one pavilion are located the Fire and Police Departments, with cells for the detention of prisoners; in another, the offices of the Ambulance Service, the physicians and pharmacy, the Foreign Department, and the Information Bureau; in the third, the post-office and a bank, and in the fourth the offices of Public Comfort and a restaurant. On the upper floors of the pavilions are the board-rooms, the committee-rooms, the rooms of the Director-General, the Department of Publicity and Promotion, and of the United States Columbian Commission.

Inquiry here gives you a fund of information concerning the Exposition that you have hitherto failed to acquire, and which is, now that you are on the grounds, of more than passing interest. Briefly stated, you learn, for example, that the total cost of the Exposition is something like $17,500,000. Of this amount Chicago citizens subscribed $6,000,000; the Illinois Legislature authorized the city to issue bonds for $5,000,000 more; and the United States Government contributed $1,500,000 and loaned $5,000,000. In addition to this, of course, each State, the same as each foreign country, appropriated a certain sum to provide for its own particular exhibit.

Here, too, you get information as to the dimensions and cost of the various buildings, in all probability in tabulated form something like this :—

Buildings.	Feet.		Acres.	Cost.
Manufactures	787	by 1687	30.5	$1,000,000
Agriculture	500	800	9.2	540,000
Annex	328	500	3.8	
Machinery	500	800	9.8	
Power-house	80	600	1.1	1,200,000
Annexes	490	551	6.2	
Assembly Hall	450	500	5.2	200,000
Mines and Mining	350	700	5.6	250,000
Electricity	345	700	5.5	365,000
Administration	260	260	1.6	450,000
Transportation	250	960	5.5	280,000
Horticulture	250	1000	5.8	300,000
Women's	200	400	1.8	120,000
United States Government	350	420	3.4	400,000
Navy Battle-ship	248	69	2.0	100,000
Fisheries	163	363	1.0	200,000
Annexes	135	diameter.	0.8	
Fine Arts	320	by 500	3.7	500,000
Annexes	123	200	1.1	
Forestry	200	500	2.3	100,000
Saw-mill	125	300	0.9	35,000
Dairy	95	200	0.5	30,000
Live Stock	53	330	1.3	150,000
Live Stock Sheds			40.0	
Music Hall	140	200	0.7	100,000
Restaurant	140	200	0.7	100,000
				$6,430,000

Armed with this array of figures you stop for an inspection of the under side of the dome, which you discover is enriched with deep panelings filled in with sculpture in low relief and enormous paintings, representing the arts and sciences, and then you descend to *terra firma* once more, and passing out by the northern archway, find yourself between the Mines and Mining and the Electrical Buildings. You choose the latter for your next visit, and, as is your habit, halt a moment before entering to take in at a glance some of its chief architectural features. What impresses you most forcibly is the portico and colon-

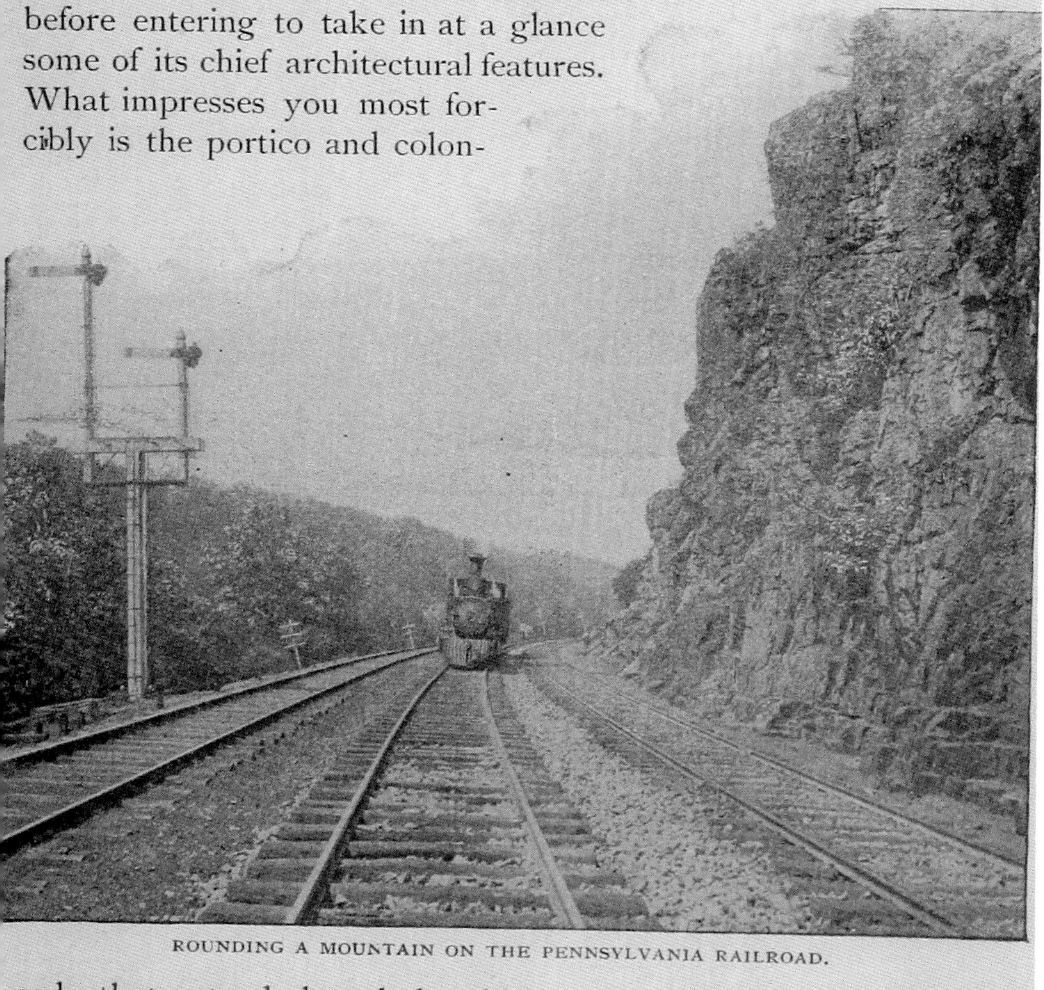

ROUNDING A MOUNTAIN ON THE PENNSYLVANIA RAILROAD.

nade that extend the whole width of the building on each side of the monumental main entrance, over which latter are inscribed a series of names famous in the annals of electrical science, and in the centre of which, upon a lofty pedestal, is a colossal statue of Benjamin Franklin, whose illustrious name connects the early history of the Republic with one of the most important discoveries in the phenomena of electricity. The main tower here, two hundred feet in height, also commands your gaze, as do the shorter and more slender ones on either side. While the walls have the same eburnean appearance as those of the other buildings on the Grand Avenue, you note an extravagance of decoration about the entrance that has not been observable elsewhere. The columns here, for instance, are of porphyry, and everywhere are great masses of gilt modeled work in relief, the object being, you learn, to afford as brilliant an effect as possible by night, when the whole structure is fairly ablaze with electric light.

The interior, which, after dark, must be dazzling in its brilliancy, contains nevertheless by daylight many exhibits of rare interest, and you spend hours here among the wonders which every step unfolds. The space set apart for and occupied by the inventions of the Wizard Edison is especially rich in marvels; and you can readily believe that the inventor has made this display the greatest achievement of his life. What you see is not only practical, but the effects are spectacular and novel as well.

In the decorations of the chief entrance to the Mines and Mining Building, gold, silver, and black are freely used as emblematical of mineral products. Sculptures symbolical of the character of the exhibits within are also prominent, and you observe that the general style of the building's architecture suggests the early Italian renaissance, somewhat freely treated. Here, too, are the inevitable corner pavilions with their low domes and their waving banners; and here, too, you find the usual arcade opening upon a loggia on the ground floor and wide gallery above. You are impressed somewhat by the marble facings of the loggia, of various kinds and hues, and then you realize that these are exhibits, and will probably have a good market value after the close of the Exposition.

So rich is the United States in natural mineral resources of almost every kind, and so large and varied are its requirements, that you are not surprised to find on the floor of this structure, and in the United States section, an exceedingly extensive display of all varieties of raw mineral products; of metals obtained from the ores, manufactured metals, mining and metallurgical machinery, and, indeed, everything that serves to illustrate the vast industries of mining and of metallurgy.

You discover that the subject of coal has been treated in very broad lines, the exhibit in this respect being qualitative rather than quantitative. Here are the different varieties, produced at different localities, together with the chemical analysis of each, and the results of tests determining their economic value and adaptability to various purposes. The iron exhibit, too, is arranged with full appreciation of the magnitude and importance of the iron industry; and the process of extracting the precious metals is demonstrated in the most thorough manner. One of the most interesting displays is a collection of the implements used by the pioneers who went to California in 1849, at the outbreak of the gold fever there, including an old "placer" plant in complete operation. Nor is this all. A little farther on you come upon the shafts of a coal mine, and are told that here is a full-sized model showing how coal is mined in Pennsylvania; while not far away is a similar model of an iron mine, with all the mining paraphernalia in full view.

The view from the northern end of the Mines and Mining Building, looking across the archipelago of small islands to the larger wooded island beyond, is in striking contrast with the scene you have just left, and you stand for some minutes enjoying the sylvan prospect before turning to your left and entering the golden portal of the Transportation Building, which here stretches its length of nine hundred and sixty feet along the western edge of the Jackson Park site. Romanesque in general style, it, nevertheless, in some particulars—the manner in which it is designed on axial lines, the solicitude shown for fine proportions, and the subtle relation of parts to each other—suggests the methods of composition followed at the Ecole des Beaux Arts. The golden door, through an immense single arch, enriched to an extraordinary degree with carvings, bas reliefs, and several paintings, chief among which is a modeled representation of the passenger train *par excellence* of the world—the Pennsylvania Limited—which has a place directly over the entrance, is the keynote of the eastern front, and the remainder of the architectural composition falls into a just relation of contrast with it, consisting of a continuous arcade, with subordinated colonnade and entablature. There are, too, you see, numerous minor entrances, grouped about which are terraces sloping to the water's edge, picturesque seats, convenient drinking fountains, and beautiful statuary, all of which, taken with the red and yellow and gold of the exterior decorations, the blue-green of the lagoon, and the rich foliage and flowers of the island opposite, compose a picture more rich in color than is to be found anywhere else on the grounds.

The interior of the building reveals a treatment similar to that of a Roman basilica, with broad nave and aisles. The roof is in three divisions, the middle one rising much higher than the others, and with its walls pierced to form a beautiful arcade clere-story. To the cupola, which is in the exact centre of the building, you may ascend by any one of eight elevators, themselves exhibits, and from the height of one hundred and sixty-five feet get a view of the park and its ornaments entirely different from any you have yet had.

In the way of exhibits, you find about every object that will illustrate the work of transportation, whether by land, water, or air ; and observe that the collection has been given a historic as well as practical interest by the introduction of examples of the earliest and crudest forms of transportation appliances from all parts of the world. Off from the northwest corner of the Transportation Building proper you stray into what is called the Service Building, an annex covering nine acres, wherein you discover a stupendous array of railway trains, including engines and cars. At least a hundred locomotives are facing the central avenue, and the perspective is fine beyond description.

The rose-tinted Horticultural Building, with its crystal domes and roofs, and its many windows of flashing glass, reflecting its own showy banners and the trees and flowers of its neighboring island, lies directly to the north of you—a great conservatory a thousand feet in length and with a maximum width of two hundred and eighty-seven feet, surrounded by grounds laid out in the most elaborate manner known to the art of the landscape gardener. Grounds garnished with fountains and statuary, huge vases containing flowers in bloom, tanks in which grow the Egyptian lotus and other specimens of nympheas, all sloping to a low parapet that rises above a spacious landing stage on the shore of the lagoon.

Once inside the building you traverse a long court, beautifully decorated in color and planted with ornamental shrubs and flowers ; stand spell-bound beneath the central dome, into which mount enormously tall palms, bamboos, tree ferns, cacti, and eucalyptus, or climb to the galleries, and in one of the cafés there situated partake of a luncheon to the music of splashing fountains and surrounded by the sweet odors of many flowers.

The courts facing the wooded island, you note, are devoted especially to tender plants, while in the rear courts are the fruit-growing exhibits that require a cooler temperature. Here you find a large section given over exclusively to the exhibition of orange culture in California and Florida, while a most interesting exhibit, not far away, consists of the dwarf fruit and other trees of Japan, over a century old and not more than two feet high.

A few steps north of the Horticultural Building you come upon the red-roofed structure devoted to woman's work—designed by a woman and crowded with the results of woman's handicraft. Its style is the Italian renaissance, and it covers a space of two hundred by four hundred feet. It is encompassed by luxuriant shrubs and beds of fragrant flowers, and stands like a white silhouette against a background of verdant leafage. In front of it the lagoon takes the form of a bay about four hundred feet in width. From the middle of this bay a grand landing and stair-case leads to a terrace six feet above the water. Crossing this terrace, other stair-ways give access to the ground, four feet above, on which, at about one hundred feet back, the building is situated.

You enter a lobby, forty feet wide, which leads into a rotunda open to the roof, protected by a richly-ornamented skylight, and surrounded by a two-story open arcade, the effect being that of an Italian court-yard, of delicate and chaste design. On the left of the main entrance is a thoroughly equipped hospital, with women physicians and trained nurses, prepared to handle the gravest cases of accident or illness, and, adjoining this, a room filled with couches and hospital beds—a branch of the Department of Public Comfort—for such cases of indisposition as do not require serious or regular medical attention. On your right, as you enter the building, is a model kindergarten, with all the latest improvements for the education of the infant mind. In the south pavilion you find what is described as the "Retrospective Exhibit," and in the north pavilion everything that relates to reform work and charity organization.

Upstairs, in the second story, are the ladies' parlors, committee-rooms, and dressing-rooms, all leading to the open balcony in front. Adjoining these on one side is a great assembly room, while on the other are located a model kitchen and refreshment rooms. Above this floor, open to the air and surrounded by a supplementary colonnade, are the hanging gardens, which give to the building, from the outside, somewhat the appearance of a Pompeiian villa.

Having given yourself a thorough idea of the work of which woman is capable, you proceed to an inspection of the largest of the individual State buildings on the grounds, that of Illinois, which lies a little to the north on a piece of land surrounded on three sides by the waters of the system of lagoons. In size it is four hundred by one hundred and sixty feet, and in style severely classic, with a dome in the centre and a great porch facing southward. The interior, save for a space at one end reserved for a model school-house, is an unbroken rectangular hall, crowded with exhibits of the States' products and specialties. Now, for a time, you stroll about among the pavilions of the various States and Territories which are grouped in this part of the grounds, and which in their varied architectural features present a strong contrast to the larger structures at the southern end of the park, which, as you have observed, all bear a family resemblance. Wisconsin's building, for example, which you pass soon after leaving the Illinois building, is merely a Queen Anne cottage, three stories in height; while on the space allotted to Florida, near the northern extremity of the grounds, is a full-sized reproduction of old Fort Marion, which was built at St. Augustine in 1620, and which is believed to be the oldest building in the United States. This structure, you conclude, is well worth inspection. It is, you learn, made of frame, but being covered with the phosphate rock of Florida it has the appearance of stone. Surrounding the fort is a moat, part of which is arranged as a sunken garden, in which you see growing the tropical plants of the State—the pine-apple, banana, rice, sugar cane, oranges, &c., while in another portion, filled with water, you get a glimpse of several alligators and crocodiles. The buildings of New York and Pennsylvania are, as a matter of course, somewhat pretentious, but a number of the smaller States, you note, have contented themselves with French chateaus, Swiss chalets, and a dozen and one other all too common forms of construction.

Now the pure Grecian Ionic architecture of the Fine Arts Building comes before you as a relief from the conglomerate collection of styles through which you have just passed. Its cool, light-gray walls and its brilliant blue dome, standing out from among groups of statues—replica ornaments of classic art—which adorn the grounds, are enhanced in beauty by the contrast, and you approach the structure with all the devotion and reverence that Art should command. Climbing one of the four broad flights of steps that lead to the sculptured portals, you enter a vestibule, the walls of which are adorned with paintings illustrating the history and progress of the arts. These you find extend also through the nave which runs the length of the building, and through the transept which divides the rectangle into four large galleries. In these passage-ways, too, are the exhibits of statuary and other sculpture. The four large galleries, and several smaller courts off from these, are devoted entirely to paintings—one of the larger courts being filled with the United States' art exhibit ; another with the pictures of English artists ; the third with German art works ; and the fourth with the magnificent display made by the Republic of France. When you have exhausted the pictures in which this building abounds you visit the annexes that are located to the east and the west, where you find an additional display of canvasses, water-colors, etchings, engravings, and architectural drawings gathered from the four corners of the globe.

Between these art palaces, which, in view of their valuable contents, are the most substantially built of all the Exposition edifices, and the Fisheries Building, located about a thousand feet in a straight line to the south, are to be seen some of the principal foreign buildings, including those of Great Britain, Germany, France, Italy, Russia, Spain, Mexico, and some of the South American Republics. Here you find the fine old-looking English manor house—is it Hatfield or Sandringham?—with its spacious armor-hung hall and its model garden. Here also are an ancient-appearing German castle; an Aztec temple, such as one sees in various parts of Mexico; and, on the plot assigned to Ecuador, a reproduction of the Incas' "Temple of the Sun," that you remember to have seen at the Paris Exposition of 1889.

The Fisheries Building, which you now visit, is a somewhat ornate affair in the Spanish-Romanesque style, colored in imitation of the Cordova Cathedral, the archivalts being picked out in red blocks on a dull buff

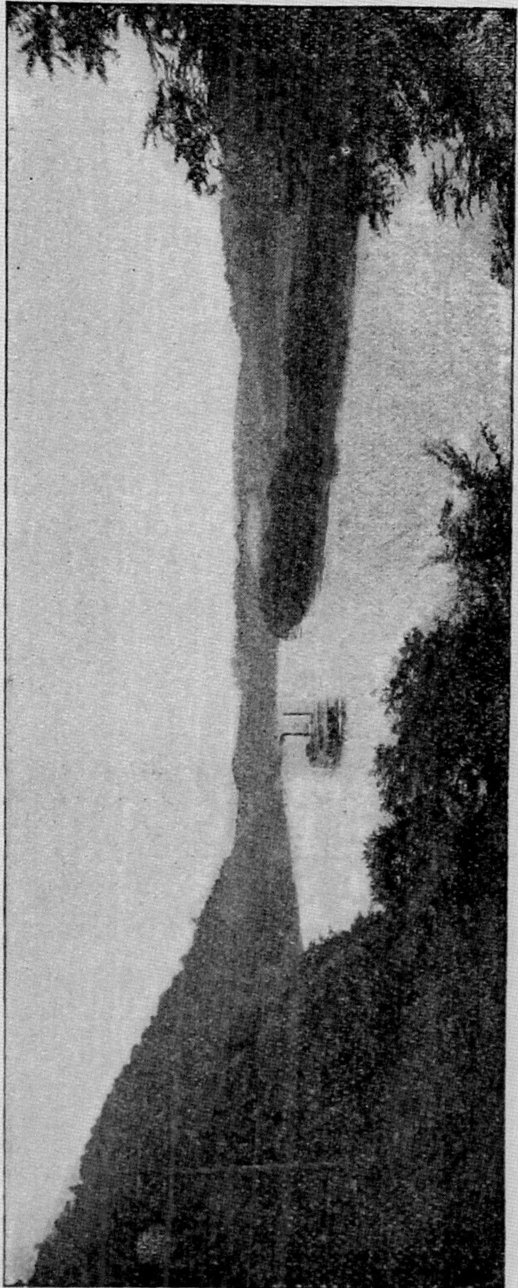

ON THE MONONGAHELA RIVER.

ground, and the roofs appropriately painted a marine blue. In the centre of the main building is located a large basin or pool, from which rises a towering mass of rocks, covered with moss and lichens, and from the crevices of which gush crystal streams of water which drop to the reeds, rushes, and ornamental semi-aquatic plants in the basin below. Here gorgeous golden ides, golden trench, and other golden fishes disport themselves. From this point, too, you get a view of one side of the larger series of aquaria, ten in number, and having a capacity of from seven thousand to twenty-seven thousand gallons of water each. Here, also, are numerous cases containing models of fish of all kinds and from every clime. Passing out of the rotunda you reach a great corridor or arcade, where on one hand you view the opposite side of the series of great tanks, and on the other a line of tanks somewhat smaller, ranging in capacity from seven hundred and fifty to fifteen hundred gallons, making together a panorama that rivals that to be seen in any great permanent aquarium of the world. Part of these large tanks you notice are under ground, and as you stand watching you see rise up from the bottom an enormous shark, sword-fish, or some other mighty denizen of the deep. In the annex on the other side of the rotunda you find an angling exhibit, including all sorts of fishing paraphernalia, comprising rods, reels, nets, boats, &c. In this structure, too, are shown the methods of fish hatching and fish cultivation.

Crossing the bay which skirts the Fisheries Building on the south the United States Government Building and grounds lie directly before you. The structure, you observe, is large and imposing, but by no means overburdened with ornaments. Rectangular in plan, its centre is surmounted by an eight-sided dome, from which flies the Stars and Stripes of the Union, and its main entrance is beneath an heroic, sculpture-crowned arch of the triumphal order. Entering here you find yourself in the midst of a most interesting display. In the northern half are the exhibits of the Fisheries Commission, the Smithsonian Institute, and the Interior Department, while in the southern half you discover the exhibits of the Post-Office Department, Treasury Department, War Department, and Department of Agriculture. The United States Mint authorities show not only a complete collection of the coins of the United States, but a very excellent collection of the coins of foreign countries as well; the Supervising Architect of the Treasury shows a number of photographs of the public buildings and parks at Washington, the Bureau of Engraving and Printing displays a complete collection of the paper money of the United States, and the Quartermaster's Department exhibits lay-figure officers and men of all grades in the army, mounted and on foot, and fully equipped in the uniforms of their rank and service. In this same section you see nineteen figures showing the uniforms worn during the Revolutionary War and the War of 1812, and thirty-one figures showing the uniforms worn in the Mexican War. Here, also, is an exhibition of how the telephone is used on the battle-field, together with a showing of all the means of army telegraphing and signaling.

In the Patent Office exhibit you come across a comprehensive array of models illustrating the wonderful progress of mechanical civilization, one group showing the development of the printers' art, from Guttenberg's crude invention to the latest rotary perfecting and folding printing press, and others demonstrating in similar manner the evolution of the steam engine, sewing machine, &c.

On the grounds of the Government Building, which are quite extensive, you find, aside from the army encampment and the exhibit of the Ordnance Department—consisting of huge guns and explosives—a life-saving station, built and equipped with every appliance, and manned by a crew giving practical exhibitions of the work done by this heroic branch of the service.

But what interests you, probably, most of all is the exhibit here under cover, made by the Coast Survey, of a huge model of the United States, fully four hundred feet square, on a scale showing the exact height of the mountains, the length and depth of the rivers, and the curvature of the earth. This you view from galleries built around it, and from elevated pathways over which you travel the length and breadth of the country.

The Naval exhibit, on board the full-sized model of a coast-line battle-ship, is the next object that claims your attention, and you walk past the snowy tents of the soldiers, the neatly-kept quarters of the life-saving guard, and the frowning guns of the Ordnance Department to the white promenade that borders the lake, where you stop to view at this distance the long white hull with its many port-holes and its belligerent-looking armament, from the midst of which rises its single mast, circled by two tops or balconies, over whose guards are pointing small rapid-firing guns. On the starboard side you see the rigging of the torpedo protection net, stretching the entire length of the vessel, while steam launches and cutters riding at the booms give to the whole all the outward appearance of a real ship of war. That it is not a real ship, but only a model built of brick and concrete on a submerged platform in the lake, is due, you learn, to an old treaty between the United States and Great Britain forbidding either power to have more than one war-ship on the lakes; and this one, of course, has so much to do that it would be out of all reason to expect it to anchor here for exhibition purposes.

Aboard the model, which has been named the *Illinois*, you find that it is not only a war-ship in outward appearance, but in interior fitting as well. A detail of officers, seamen, mechanics, and marines man the vessel, and as you go on board you discover that a torpedo drill is in progress. An inspection of the battery shows you that it comprises four 13-inch breech-loading rifle cannon, eight 8-inch breech-loading rifle cannon, four 6-inch breech-loading rifle cannon, twenty 6-pounder rapid-firing guns, six 1-pounder rapid-firing guns, two Gatling guns, and six torpedo tubes or torpedo guns. Below are the cabins, state-rooms, lavatories, latrines, mess-rooms, galleys, lockers, and berthings, giving an admirable idea how the men live on board a man-of-war; while from the conning tower above you get a very fair notion of how the commander of such a ship views an engagement in which he has entered and communicates his orders to the different parts of the vessel. As for the traditional naval uniforms from 1775 to 1848, you see them upon living models.

Hailing a small boat from the top of one of the ladders that descend from the deck to the water's edge, you employ the boatman to convey you, by way of the bays and canals, across the Fair grounds to the Woman's Building again, whence you proceed on foot through the beautiful gardens surrounding this structure to the beginning of that strip of land, six hundred feet in width and a mile long, called the Midway Plaisance, which you find crowded with a congregation of bazaars of all nations. If you were at Paris in 1889 it is sure to remind you of the Rue de Caire, though, as is everything here, it is on a very much larger scale. In order to get a general view of this cosmopolitan avenue, you decide to begin by riding from one end of it to the other, and accordingly board one of the trains of the sliding water railway that attracted so much attention at the Paris Exposition, and that are said to be capable of making a speed of something like two hundred miles an hour. No such momentum as this, however, is here attempted, but you are carried swiftly and smoothly over the polished rails, and arrive at the other end of the avenue with a confused impression of gorgeous marquees, picturesque kivaks, stately castles, ruined temples, hospitable posadas, gaily-colored theatres, long, cool-looking bungalows, and a host of other structures. Now as you start to walk back you are jostled by types of people from all the countries of the earth—the stalwart red Indian, wrapped in his blanket, emotionless as a stone, and concealing his wonder beneath a stolidity that you admire but cannot equal; the small, but alert, Japanese, with his loose dress caught up as if it were an obstacle that he would fain dispense with; the almond-eyed Chinaman, with his braided queue; the turbaned Turk; the Egyptian, with his inevitable red fez; the brilliantly-uniformed attachés of the European commissions; the cool, white-clothed, and Panama-hatted hidalgo from Mexico or one of the Spanish-peopled countries of South America, and ordinary-looking folk like yourself from here, there, and everywhere.

Among the more interesting features of this part of the Exposition, where an extra price of admission is charged, and where, for the first time in your tour of the grounds, you find exhibits for sale as well as for show, you note a reproduction on a grand scale of the Tower of London, with its many historic associations, and through which you are shown by a robust Englishman in the costume of a Beef-eater. A little farther on you come across the Guatemala exhibit of one of the palaces of the ruined city of Antigua; and not far away is the Capitol Building of the United States of Columbia, in miniature. A colony of the lace-makers and the gold and silver workers of Paraguay claims your attention for a moment, and then you pass on to where the celebrated Pandure family, from the State of Guadalajara in Mexico, living in a thorougly Mexican dwelling, are working in clay and modeling figures that would do credit to a master sculptor.

An East Indian and a Turkish street are here, showing not only the wares peculiar to the country, but the mechanics, artisans, and professional entertainers. Here Egypt has reproduced one of Cairo's chief avenues, four hundred feet in length, lined with shops, cafés, dwellings, and amusement halls, and peopled with donkey-drivers, Egyptian serving-maids, dancing girls, jugglers, merchants, women, and children. Japan, also, has a village picturing her architecture and scenes from her home-life. China, exhibiting for the first time with the sanction of her government, presents to your gaze wonders hitherto never seen outside of the Flowery Kingdom, and Persia shows you a street that recalls memories of tales from the Arabian Nights. Beside all this you are confronted on every side by panoramas, captive balloons, fountains of native wines, coal palaces and corn palaces, and, what is by no means the least interesting part of this wonderful section of the Exposition, a portion of a gigantic red-wood tree from California that stood three hundred and ninety feet high, and was twenty-six feet in diameter, now leveled and divided, its trunk hollowed out, and the interior fashioned into full-sized railway cars, fitted in the style of Pullman coaches of the latest and most approved design. In one forty-five-foot length you find a sleeping car, with berths closed and berths made-up ; and in another a dining car similar to those used on the Pennsylvania Railroad, with a kitchen and all its appurtenances.

Now the day is nearly done, and the tops of the buildings are crimsoned by the setting sun. Far away, down the grounds, the dome of the Administration Palace is a great molten ball of flame, and the glass domes of some of the other structures are dazzling as mammoth gems, glittering with all the prismatic colors. Ten minutes more and the light has paled ; night's black robe is falling, and threatens to envelop everything in its dusky folds, when suddenly, on all sides, from one extreme boundary of the park to the other, a million lights flash into brilliant being, and once more, though the skies be dark above, the avenues and water-ways of the vast inclosure are as luminous as at noonday. Having seen the Exposition by daylight, you linger now to see it again in all the spectacular glory of its electrical illumination. You climb, perhaps, to the hanging gardens of the Woman's Pavilion, and from there let your gaze sweep southward over the great artificially-lighted area, thus getting a bird's-eye view that is well worth your while; or it is possible that you engage one of those funereal-looking gondolas and drift lazily through the lagoons, whose depths are lighted with electric lamps arranged beneath the waters. A cool breeze from the lake fans your cheeks; to your ears comes the music of the great orchestra playing some dreamy waltz, and as you loll back on your cushions you see darting here and there through the transparent depths below you curiously-shaped and colored artificial fishes and marine monsters, lighted and propelled by the electric currents.

You remember that at Paris but three of the buildings were open in the evening. Here every one of the great halls is open and aglow with light. In all but the Fine Arts, the Administration, and the Woman's Building arc lights are employed. In Machinery Hall there are six hundred; in Agricultural Hall, six hundred; in the Electric Building, four hundred; in the Mines and Mining Building, four hundred; in the Transportation Building, four hundred and fifty; in Horticultural Hall, four hundred; in the Forestry Building, one hundred and fifty; and in the Great Palace of the Liberal Arts, two thousand. Twelve thousand incandescent lamps light the Fine Arts Building; ten thousand more are ablaze in the Administration Building; and in the Woman's Building there are one hundred and eighty arc lights and twenty-seven hundred incandescent lamps.

When at length you approach the Grand Avenue the scene becomes more and more beautiful. Every window and archway of the great edifices here are sending out broad columns of light, illuminated fountains are throwing aloft their brilliant-hued waters, groups of white statuary stand out in bold and striking outline against the black shadows, and the golden ornaments of the entrances to the several mammoth piles facing the Grand Canal flash and glitter in the flood of dazzling effulgence.